From Couch to Conditioned:
A Beginner's Guide to Getting Fit

Pilates
for Beginners

DENIS KENNEDY, SIAN WILLIAMS, AND DOMINIQUE JANSEN

ROSEN
PUBLISHING®

New York

This edition published in 2012 by:

The Rosen Publishing Group, Inc.
29 East 21st Street
New York, NY 10010

Additional end matter copyright © 2012 by The
Rosen Publishing Group, Inc.

**Library of Congress Cataloging-in-
Publication Data**

Kennedy, Denis.
Pilates for beginners / Denis Kennedy, Sian
Williams, Dominique Jansen.
    p. cm.—(From couch to conditioned: a
beginner's guide to getting fit)
Includes bibliographical references and index.
ISBN 978-1-4488-4815-7 (library binding)
ISBN 978-1-4488-4819-5 (pbk.)
ISBN 978-1-4488-4823-2 (6-pack)
1. Pilates method—Juvenile literature.
I. Williams, Siân, Dr. II. Jansen, Dominique.
III. Title. IV. Title. V. Series.
RA781.4.K46 2012
613.7'192—dc22
                            2011010687

Manufactured in the United States of America

CPSIA Compliance Information: Batch #S11YA: For further
information, contact Rosen Publishing, New York, New York, at
1-800-237-9932.

contents

foreword BY JILLIAN HESSEL

The Pilates Method has come a very long way since 1981, when I took my first class with Kathy Grant, a student of Joseph Pilates himself. At this time, Pilates was popular with professional dancers and a handful of other people "in the know," but was mostly unknown to the outside world. I was a professional dancer with an injured back. Word of mouth led me to Kathy's Studio, located in Henri Bendel's department store in Manhattan. Fortunately, fate had led me to one of the best teachers ever trained by Joseph Pilates, or "Papa Joe" as he was known to his students. Through Kathy's constant encouragement and careful coaching, my back got better and I was able to continue my dance career—a small miracle!

However, Kathy also encouraged me to learn to teach Pilates' work. As there were no formal training programs at the time, she sent me to train to teach with her colleague Carola Trier. Carola was a German expatriate, like Papa Joe himself, and she ran a large, busy studio not far from Kathy's place. Thus began an interesting apprenticeship: I would train to teach with Carola in the morning, and walk across town to Kathy's in the afternoon. I had to learn to be flexible, because though the root and essence of Pilates' work remained the same, Carola and Kathy had completely different teaching styles and personalities.

The gift that I carry with me today from the unique training I received from these two remarkable women is that there is not just one way to work with a student, or to teach a Pilates exercise. In the past 20 years, I have gone on to study with as many of the Pilates

Master Teachers as I could, all of whom were taught by Joseph Pilates himself: I have taken workshops with Eve Gentry and Romana Kryzanowa, and Ron Fletcher, in particular, has had an indelible influence on my teaching style. No matter who the teacher, though, the message is always the same: though the specifics of a particular exercise (the "choreography") may differ, the fundamental principles of Pilates—which you will learn in this book—remain unchanged.

I am delighted to write the foreword for *Pilates for Beginners*, because the authors have taken the time to educate the reader about the Pilates Method and its six fundamental principles. Then, they explain the pre-Pilates exercises, or "warm-ups," as Kathy Grant used to call them, before demonstrating Classic Pilates work, along with sensible modifications, which occur throughout the exercise program.

This book provides an excellent introduction to the Pilates Method, and presents the material in a logical sequence that makes it accessible, practical, and fun. So as Carola Trier used to say: "It's time to get going!"

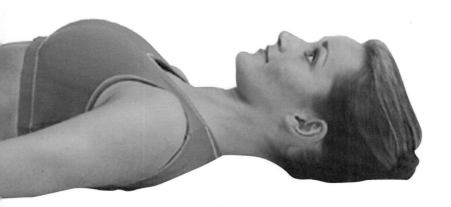

1

getting started

This first chapter looks at getting started with your Pilates training. You will find out how to assess your current level of fitness and how a Pilates exercise routine can fit in with your lifestyle. The chapter also looks at finding classes and a teacher, then at what can be achieved with Pilates, before moving on to discuss some of the equipment that can be used during your Pilates practice.

self-assessment

Before you embark on the Pilates approach to exercise, you should ask yourself a few simple questions about your health and general fitness to help you figure out exactly what you are aiming to achieve. The questions below have been designed so that you can assess your current levels of health and fitness.

if you are pregnant
If you are pregnant, then you need to find a class with a teacher who is qualified to teach Pilates for pregnancy, rather than trying to start doing the exercises alone. Pilates is a wonderful form of exercise to do both throughout pregnancy and certainly after birth, but you will need remedial adaptations of the original exercises. As a postnatal form of exercise it is excellent, but do check with your doctor that you are ready to start a program of exercise before beginning. As a general rule of thumb, do not start a class until six weeks after giving birth, and at least 12 weeks after a cesarean section. Once you have been given the go-ahead, you will find Pilates one of the best possible

ANSWER THESE QUESTIONS

1	Are you pregnant?	**2**	Have you ever had surgery (and, if so, for what)?

DO YOU SUFFER NOW, OR HAVE YOU SUFFERED IN THE PAST, FROM ANY OF THE FOLLOWING CONDITIONS:

3	Heart disease—are you on medication?	**8**	Strained or torn ligaments?
4	Respiratory problems, such as asthma?	**9**	Injured knees?
5	A serious digestive disorder such as inflammatory bowel disease (IBD) or colitis?	**10**	Whiplash?
6	Pain involving the back, the neck, and/or the shoulders?	**11**	Bulging or herniated disks?
		12	Broken bones?
7	Fractured bones?	**13**	Repetitive strain injury?

If the answer to any of these questions is "yes," it does not mean you cannot follow a program of Pilates exercises, but you should speak to your doctor, or other health professional, before starting.

ways of regaining abdominal muscle strength and general allover body tone.

choosing your exercise level

The exercises included in this program range from the very simple to an intermediate level of difficulty in order to help you build your strength and flexibility at a pace that suits you. If you have not exercised for some time, or if you are recovering from an injury or illness, you should keep to the simpler exercises until you feel strong enough to undertake the more complicated movements. Each exercise in this program will be clearly marked as "beginner" or "intermediate" level. Try to be honest with yourself about your current state of fitness and general health, and think about what exactly you wish to improve.

- Do your joints feel very stiff in the mornings/does your back ache after standing up for prolonged periods?
- Does your head ache after a day sitting at the computer?
- Would you like to be more energetic, have stronger abdominals, or have more flexibility?
- How motivated are you to try to achieve these goals?

By being realistic and committing yourself to a minimum of a twice-weekly Pilates workout, you will soon feel fitter,

JUDGING YOUR FITNESS

So, the next issue to tackle is: how fit are you at this moment?

1	Do you get breathless climbing the stairs?
2	Do you drive everywhere rather than walk?
3	Are you overweight?
4	How much aerobic activity do you get in a week?
5	Do you do any other forms of exercise, such as dancing, running, going to the gym, playing golf, tai chi, swimming, yoga, martial arts?
6	What is your diet like? Do you eat fresh fruit and vegetables regularly, or do you live on "fast" food?

healthier, and more mobile. Pilates is the perfect body-conditioning technique for incorporating into any general exercise regime, whether you like to walk, jog, play sports, swim, or dance. It teaches good breathing habits, correct postural alignment, and improved body awareness. All of this information will enable you to get the most out of everything you do.

finding time for pilates

You should also think about how much time you have available for exercise. Again, it is wise to be honest and realistic about this. It is pointless to tell yourself that you will go swimming four times a week, walk everywhere, and do three Pilates classes when the reality is that you work long hours and have limited free time, or have children to get to and from school, after-school activities to attend, and many other pressures on your time that make driving from A to B the only sensible option.

CHOOSING THE RIGHT TEACHER

1 Whether you are looking for a one-to-one mat class, a general mat class, or an equipment-based class, it is essential to find a good, well-qualified teacher.

2 A good teacher, in either a mat or studio environment, will always ask you for details of your medical history before you begin.

3 Choose a teacher who has undergone a proper training course (conducted by a recognized center), which will have involved learning functional anatomy and specific remedial adaptations for injuries.

4 Find a class that is at a convenient time and in a convenient location. If it is too difficult to get to, you won't go.

5 Avoid classes where there are more than 15 students per teacher. One of the great benefits of the Pilates approach to exercise is the attention to detail involved in getting the movements right. No teacher, no matter how wonderful, can watch and correct too many people at once.

Look at the structure of your days and see where you can make time to fit in a Pilates workout. A typical full-length Pilates class lasts between 60 and 90 minutes, but the beauty of the technique is that a smaller program of, say, 20 minutes carried out more frequently can be highly beneficial too. You decide what best fits in with your lifestyle, without making yourself more stressed by trying to do too much.

The likelihood is that as you get fitter and healthier you will have more energy and be able to fit in more exercise without wearing yourself out or increasing your stress levels. Remember, exercise undertaken in a stressful, forced way is as unhealthy for your body and soul as no exercise at all.

the basics

You need to combine various elements in your lifestyle if you are to become as healthy as possible. Hopefully, the fitness questionnaire on the previous page will have made you aware of some of these. For example, what you put into your body is as crucial to its well-being as how you use it physically. Eating a healthy, balanced diet that includes lots of fresh fruit, vegetables, protein, and water helps to create the right framework for a healthy body. If you are concerned about your diet, consult your doctor for advice on the right foods to eat, or ask the doctor to recommend a qualified local dietitian.

common sense is best

Following the latest food fads or "yo-yo" dieting (where you alternate between eating very little and binge eating) has a negative effect on your metabolism and reduces the efficiency with which your body converts food into energy.

Different body types need different levels and types of nutrients in order to function at their best. In addition, many people have dietary disorders, such as an allergy to certain types of food. If you are unsure exactly what is best for you, a professional consultation would be a good idea.

However, when it comes to lifestyle, common sense is often your best resource. For example, a healthy body needs regular sleep. So, if you routinely suffer from broken sleep you should take steps to find out why:

- Do you drink coffee, or some other caffeine drink, just before bed?
- Do you have one too many glasses of wine in the evening?
- Do you leap straight into bed from work or when you have been out for the evening, without allowing yourself a "wind-down" period?

Think about how you live your life and decide whether there is room for change. Make time and space for yourself to think, relax, exercise, to eat well, to get as much sleep as you need, to drink lots of water and less coffee and tea, and you will be on your way to a less stressed, more alert state.

matwork classes

The basic Pilates program is designed to be performed without equipment, although you can use various accessories, such as an exercise mat, Swiss ball, resistance band, or hand and leg weights, to enhance the effectiveness of the exercises. Several different types of Pilates classes are available. For example, you could choose a matwork format in which you work out with a others on mats on the floor, following the sort of program described in this book.

Matwork classes such as these are usually easier to find than equipment-based studio classes because they require only a large-enough room and a mat. They are often less expensive than equipment-based classes, too, as less supervision is required. You can also arrange for an instructor to come to your home to teach a mat class.

equipment classes

Pilates can also be taught on a range of specially designed equipment, which uses spring-resistance and pulley systems to increase and enhance the range of options for the exercises. Classes are typically much smaller than mat classes and each client follows a program tailored to meet his or her needs. If you are injured or recovering from serious illness, this type of class will be more appropriate than a general mat class, because the teacher will be able to adapt the exercises to make them safe and appropriate for your condition, and monitor you with care.

how to start

Once you have carried out a self-assessment on your general health, and established how much time you can devote to Pilates exercises, you will want to know how you go about it.

• How often should you work out?

• What kind of clothing is suitable for a workout?

• Do you need specialized equipment?

• If you decide to take it further, what types of supervised classes are available, and where do you go to find a good teacher?

Most people find that performing a Pilates workout two or three times a week gives the best results. However, once a week will do if you manage to include a reasonable number of other physical activities. It is particularly important that you carry out some sort of regular aerobic activity in addition to your Pilates program. This is because Pilates alone will not improve your cardiovascular fitness, especially at the beginners' stage. Think of Pilates as giving you structural fitness, while fast walking, running, swimming, or any other energetic exercise that raises your heart rate but can be sustained for 20 minutes or more, will provide aerobic fitness. The happiest, healthiest bodies need both.

Sportswear comes in a variety of colors, styles, and scientifically innovative fabrics. However, all that matters is that your clothes fit and you feel comfortable.

Choose a top that offers you the right level of warmth and sufficient freedom of movement.

WHAT YOU NEED

When exercising, you should wear comfortable, non-restrictive clothing that allows you to move easily and that keeps you warm without letting you get too hot.

1 Natural fibers such as cotton are preferable to synthetics, but most modern sportswear includes some Lycra because of its "stretchy" properties, and it is useful to be able to see the shape of your body so that you can check your position and alignment +as you exercise.

2 Working in bare feet is preferable as many nerve endings are located in the soles of the feet. The sensory nerves pick up information through contact and touch with the floor. Therefore working with bare feet creates a higher level of sensitivity.

3 Use free weights for exercises involving isolated arm and leg work, up to a maximum of 3 lb (1.5 kg).

Weights can either be held in the hands (as below) or strapped around the wrists or ankles (right).

Yoga mats provide a comfortable non-slip surface on which to exercise.

2

the six pilates principles

As you will see, Pilates is much more than just a simple exercise routine. It is a carefully constructed practice that emphasizes the connection between mind and body. This union is achieved through the six basic principles detailed in this chapter: breathing, concentration, center, precision, flow, and control. Each of the principles is accompanied by exercises to demonstrate fully the practice behind the theory.

finding balance

The Pilates Method is a form of structural fitness program. Its main goal is to achieve a "balanced body." The term "balanced" is relative and depends on the age, health, and structure of the individual. There is no such thing as an ideal body, let alone an ideal shape. We're all slightly different in terms of size, build, strength, and flexibility. So, in order to achieve balance, you'll need to work with what you have.

To change "imbalance" to "balance," you have to apply your mind to your body. This is not as strange as it may seem. The skeleton is moved by muscles and the muscles are controlled by

THE BODY/MIND CONNECTION

The body/mind connection in Pilates is achieved by following basic principles. There are six main principles and numerous additional ones that are the key to performing the exercises successfully.

1 BREATHING

Good breathing technique is essential for good health and posture. Only by understanding the anatomy of breathing can we gain true physical awareness.

2 CONCENTRATION

Pilates recognized the value of clearing the mind prior to physical activity. He believed that emotional and psychological states could not be isolated from the physical.

3 CENTER

All Pilates exercises start from a stable physical center (see pp. 25 and 30–31), which must be located and maintained throughout.

4 PRECISION

The goal of each Pilates exercise is very specific, and as a result the details of each exercise must be executed in a precise fashion.

5 FLOW

It is important to keep movement and breath flowing. This avoids tension, tightness, and discomfort.

6 CONTROL

The aim of Pilates is to achieve control of mind, body, and movement. Control, however, should not be limiting or obsessive.

The additional principles could add up to a rather long list, as the Method is constantly evolving, but the most important are coordination, relaxation, and stamina. Each of the six principles should be apparent when carrying out a Pilates exercise. Only when this is so can you be sure that an exercise will be effective and structurally beneficial.

nerves. You access your nervous system by consciously applying your mind. Only then can you correct "dysfunctional movements" and "holding patterns." What these terms mean is explained later in this chapter.

The Pilates Method is a form of "mindful" exercise. There are many other forms of mindful exercise, including the Alexander Technique, Feldenkrais, Gyrotonic, Gyrokinesis, the martial arts, and above all, yoga. All have their own aims and focus. None is intended purely as exercise for exercise sake.

Many of these methods focus on the internal organs, lymphatic system, nervous system, energy pathways, and even the spiritual aspects of the body. Pilates focuses primarily on the body's structural aspects—muscles, joints, posture, and functional movements— and their link with the mind. As Pilates focuses so directly on the physical matter of the body and aims to be

anatomically sound, it makes a great foundation for other types of physical activity. The Method teaches students how their own bodies function. This awareness is then applied to other physical pursuits. The key to physical awareness is the integration of body and mind.

This chapter will explore the principles in detail and explain how they link up. In some cases, an exercise is provided as an example to help explain a principle or clarify its aims. The first principle, "Breathing," is explored in greatest depth as it is crucial to the successful performance of Pilates.

The six main principles of Pilates combine to create a structural fitness program that can achieve a truly balanced body.

principle 1: breathing

Clearly, breathing is vital to health and well-being. It is the very essence of life. Without breath there is no oxygen, no rhythm, and no life force. By learning the anatomy of breathing you will understand why the breath is crucial to the good practice of Pilates and the physical benefits it can provide. A basic understanding of—and feeling for—one's own anatomy develops physical awareness and so augments functional movement.

The diagrams in this book are designed to support the text and enable readers to visualize the way the body functions. Visualization is an important learning tool in the building of physical awareness. Combining theoretical—mental learning with physical exploration encourages mind and body integration. But it is the physical exploration that is most important; the theory is only there to help.

the anatomy of breathing

The diaphragm is the deepest of the "primary" muscles involved in breathing. It is dome-shaped and hangs like a parachute attached to the base of the ribs, breastbone, and spine. The diaphragm separates the chest (thoracic) cavity from the belly (abdominal) cavity. The lungs rest on top of the diaphragm and the digestive and reproductive organs are situated below. These organs are joined to the diaphragm by connective tissue (fascia).

The rhythm of the breath and the subsequent movement of the diaphragm set the rhythm of the heart and the squeezing (peristaltic) movements of the gut. Good breathing technique is essential for good health, and good posture creates space to allow the diaphragm and lungs to move freely, and so facilitates efficient breathing.

The diaphragm does not act alone but works in concert with the other primary respiratory muscles. Of these, the most important are the chest muscles (intercostals), the belly muscles (abdominals), and the ring of muscle that supports the bladder, rectum, and reproductive organs (pelvic-floor muscles).

As the lungs fill with air (inhalation), the diaphragm descends into the abdominal cavity and the rib cage expands. As the ribs expand, they gently rotate forward and up, much like Venetian blinds rotating to an open position. Along with the action of the ribs, the intercostals elongate, the abdominals expand, the pelvic floor descends and widens the pelvic basin, and the diaphragm shortens and extends the lower (lumbar) spine.

As the lungs expel air (exhalation), the diaphragm billows back up into the thoracic cavity, gently flexing the lumbar spine. The ribs relax back down, reducing the volume of the rib cage and automatically contracting the pelvic floor, intercostals, and abdominals.

The mechanism of the breath plays an intrinsic part in the core stability of the trunk. "Core stability," in this way, means the intrinsic support required to keep the trunk stable. There is a big difference between "stable" and "static." Stable means that the deeper skeletal muscles are working actively to stabilize and support the skeleton and that there is no "holding" and "gripping" in the outer muscles. This promotes freedom of movement with internal support, which economizes muscular effort.

location of the breath

The lungs are narrowest at the top and widen toward the bottom. This means the bottom section has much larger storage capacity and so is more efficient and economical to use during everyday activities, and in moderate exercise such as Pilates. One only needs top-lung breathing for cardiovascular activity.

The muscles that are automatically involved in top-lung breathing fatigue more easily than the primary respiratory muscles. When overused, the "top-lung muscles" tend to tighten and so inhibit efficient breathing. People who hyperventilate mainly use top-lung breathing and never empty their lower lungs fully.

In "normal" breathing, the secondary respiratory muscles are active. But on inhalation, rather than lifting and rotating the shoulder blades forward and up, they expand the chest and breastbone in order to keep the airway open and free for the passage of breath.

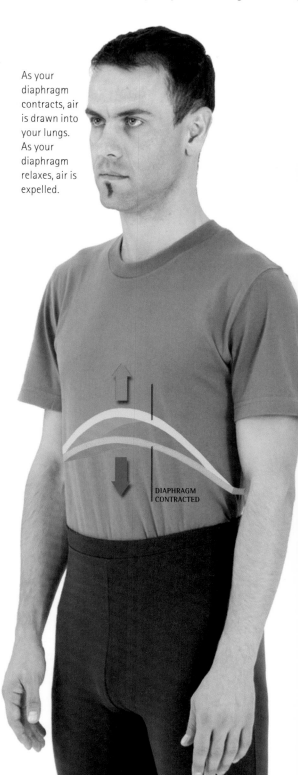

As your diaphragm contracts, air is drawn into your lungs. As your diaphragm relaxes, air is expelled.

DIAPHRAGM CONTRACTED

exploring the breath

To practice Pilates effectively, you will need to learn a lateral-breathing technique. However, before describing this technique, we will experiment with some other ways of breathing in order to understand exactly where the breath can go.

You can breathe in many ways, none of them necessarily right or wrong in all situations. They are simply ways that function best in different circumstances and at different times. Being able to direct the breath into various parts of the body augments breath control and versatility.

EXERCISE: CHEST BREATHING

1 In a comfortable seated position, place your hands on your chest.

2 On inhalation, aim to fill up the base of your lungs first, and then gradually fill the middle and top of the lungs until you have fully expanded your chest. Visualize the air widening the space between your shoulder blades, taking the shoulder blades away from your spine, opening your chest, and opening the front of your shoulders. You should be able to feel the muscles across the front of the chest, upper back, and shoulder joint, and even create an opening in the armpit. Keep your throat open and wide, like the neck of a cobra.

3 On exhalation, the breastbone and chest soften, easing gently back to the space between the shoulder blades.

EXERCISE: OCCIPITAL BREATHING

The point where the skull rests and balances on the spine is called the occiput. It is a major area of tension in the body. The musculature around the base of the skull is often very tight. It benefits from postural changes and stretches (some of which are described in The Program, pp. 50–92). Using the breath is one way of opening up this area and easing tension.

In a comfortable seated position, place your hands around the base of your skull. On inhalation, imagine your breath traveling from the base of the spine up into the base of the skull. Your throat and chest should remain easy. Your aim is to open up the back space, expanding the back of the head.

EXERCISE: ABDOMINAL BREATHING

1 Lie on your back with your knees bent and your feet and knees in line with your hips. Make sure your neck is comfortable, so that your airway is clear. If necessary, place a pillow under your head to support your neck.

2 Place your hands, one at a time, on your abdomen and inhale through your nose. Fill the bottom of your lungs, pushing your diaphragm down, expanding your abdomen, and letting the organs in your abdomen rise.

3 On exhalation, let your lungs deflate easily, allowing the air to come out through your nose or mouth. Feel how the rib cage drops and the abdomen automatically falls back toward the spine.

4 Now place your hands on either side of your lumbar spine and continue to breathe, exploring the gentle extension and bending (flexion) that occurs with the rise and fall of each breath.

EXERCISE: DIAPHRAGMATIC BREATHING

1 Lying in the same pose, place your hands on the base of your ribs and visualize the diaphragm as a dome shape at the base of the thoracic cavity.

2 On inhalation, let the diaphragm descend into the abdominal cavity, and widen at the same time so that it expands the base of the ribs as far as it can. Think of the three-dimensional aspect of a parachute: it expands forward, backward, and sideways. Try to hold a natural pose of three counts at the end of each inhalation and exhalation.

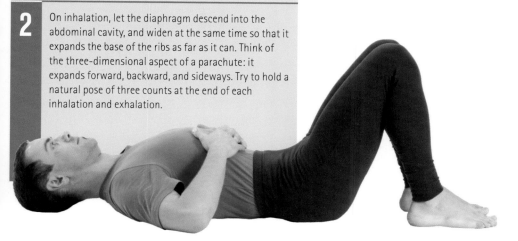

exploring the breath cont.

EXERCISE: BACK BREATHING

1 Get into a kneeling position and let your body fold forward over your thighs. Allow your entire spine to yield over. If your ankles are too tight to sit in this position, place a cushion or rolled-up towel underneath them to reduce the stretch. If your knees hurt, find a different position that allows you to achieve this method of breathing.

2 Place your hands behind your back at around the level of the kidneys. On inhalation, allow your middle and lower back to expand, opening your lower ribs like the gills of a fish.

3 On exhalation, let these imaginary gills relax back down and let the body and spine release more deeply over the thighs.

BREATHING TO STRENGTHEN THE ABDOMINALS AND LOCATE THE PELVIC FLOO

"Percussive Breathing" and "The Elevator" highlight the immediate connection between breathing and a person's internal strength. The first is a pelvic-floor exercise. The pelvic floor resides at the base of the pelvis. As well as supporting the pelvic organs, it controls the pelvic orifices. Connective tissue connects the pelvic floor to the sitting bones, the pubic bone, and the tail bone (coccyx).

Weakness in the pelvic floor can cause the pelvic organs to protrude and affect the placement and balance of the pelvis in relation to the lumbar spine, as well as having an adverse effect on abdominal strength. The following exercise, The Elevator, helps strengthen the pelvic floor and the abdominal muscles.

EXERCISE: THE ELEVATOR

1 Start this exercise in a seated position, or in a comfortable lying position with knees bent. Visualize an elevator at the base of the pelvis that travels up three floors into the lower torso. Start in the basement with your pelvic floor relaxed. The exhalation takes place in three stages, with a pause to hold the breath between each stage.

2 On the first part of the exhalation, go up to the first floor, just above your pelvis. Hold your breath and imagine some people leaving and others entering the elevator.

EXERCISE: PERCUSSIVE BREATHING

This exercise uses the breath to strengthen the abdominal muscles. It is good preparation for a classic Pilates exercise called "100s" (see pp. 66–69). 100s uses the principle that, on exhalation, the abdominals contract toward the spine and, on inhalation, they expand.

1 Lie on your back with knees bent and feet flat. Place your hands on your ribs or by your sides. You can take the exercise a little bit further by reaching your fingertips past your hips toward your feet and beating the arms gently up and down with each count while leaving space in the armpits and keeping the elbows soft.

2 Inhale through your nose and exhale through your mouth. On the exhale, let the air out in five percussive blows over a count of five, drawing the abdominals closer toward the spine with each blow.

3 Repeat for the second floor. This time the pelvic floor and abdomen pull higher up into the torso.

4 On the third stage of the exhalation, go up to the third floor, let the elevator empty, and then breathe in and let the elevator fall straight back down to the basement, fully relaxing the pelvic floor and abdomen.

3 Inhale through five counts while maintaining the abdominal contraction and sending the breath into the back. Repeat this breathing pattern 10 times, each time contracting the abdominals a little bit further and closer toward the spine.

4 Holding the abdominal contraction on the inhalation may seem to be going against nature, but it really strengthens abdominal control. If performed well, toward the end of the 10 repetitions you should feel there is hardly any space left to take in more air.

the importance of lateral breathing

The principal breathing technique used in Pilates is called "Lateral Breathing." It is important to note that the lateral-breathing technique is useful when practicing Pilates, but it is not necessarily applicable to everyday life. The technique is valid for maintaining a strong center while exercising core strength and breathing. It is not useful for walking down the street, singing, talking, and so on.

The lateral-breathing technique uses a combination of several of the ways of breathing already described. The focus is on maintaining a strong and stable abdominal center while still allowing the breath to expand the lungs and rib cage while at the same time creating a minimum of tension. The Pilates Method consistently challenges the core strength. The value of Pilates exercises is lost if you cannot support

EXERCISE: FINDING THE LATERAL BREATH

1 Come into a seated position and place your hands on the side of your ribs with your fingers pointing down toward your hips.

2 Inhale deeply. On the exhale, feel how your abdomen falls toward your spine.

3 On the next inhalation, keep the abdomen in the contracted state you felt at the end of the last inhalation and send the inhale into your hands on the sides of your ribs and the floating ribs in the back. Feel your mid-back expand out and sideways, and the lumbar spine elongating.

4 On exhalation, allow the abdomen to sink down. Feel the lumbar spine soften and the base of the ribs to fall down into the waistline.

breathing and concentration

Concentrating on your breathing and its rhythm is a perfect way to relax and empty the mind in order to create focus. Concentration means focusing on a specific activity and discarding all irrelevant thoughts. This is the next subject we will look at.

your posture and movement with a strong abdominal center. We will start by exploring lateral breathing, and then describe an exercise that allows you to apply the technique.

In this exercise, it is important to inhale via the nose and exhale via the mouth. Inhalation via the nose is important, for three reasons. First, hairs in the nostrils act as filters to cleanse the air before it enters the lungs. Second, it helps you maintain breath control, as the breath has further to go. Inhalation through the mouth uses a much shorter passage, making it harder to send the breath into the back and to control the timing of the inhalation. Third, it is easier to control the contraction of the abdominals and pelvic floor.

The reason for exhaling through the mouth is less obvious, and some Pilates exercises use either/or. However, exhaling through the mouth creates less tension in the neck and throat and gives an immediate connection with contracting the pelvic floor and abdominals. In yoga, the exhale is controlled through the nose in order to prolong the exhalation. In Pilates, this amount of prolonged control is not

EXERCISE: TABLE TOP

This exercise is a simple illustration of how to put the Lateral Breath into practice. The purpose is to use the lateral-breathing technique to stabilize the core of the body and to use the arms and legs to challenge the core.

1 Start the exercise on all fours. Try to find a neutral position of the entire spine and think "long" from the tailbone through to the crown of the head.

2 Inhale and exhale to set up the "physical center" (also referred to in this book as the "inner unit" or "power house"). To do this, simultaneously contract the abdominals, pelvic floor, and the back muscles, all creating a steady support along the core of the trunk.

3 On the next inhale, hold on to this physical center to stabilize the spine and extend one arm and the opposite leg along the floor.

4 On the next exhale, lift your arm and leg to a horizontal position.

5 Inhale, and lower the extended arm and leg back to the floor.

6 Exhale, and return to the starting position. Repeat on the other side.

necessary as the focus is on movement, not on holding and deepening the stretch of a position. Also there are many exercises in Pilates where the upper body moves by flexion and a nasal exhale might create excess tension in the neck and throat.

principle 2: concentration

Pilates requires the integration of physical and mental effort. Concentration is directly linked to this process of connecting body and mind. Without the ability to concentrate, the benefits of an exercise can easily be lost.

Joseph Pilates borrowed the principle of mental and physical body conditioning from Eastern philosophies. He recognized the importance of clearing the mind in order to carry out any physical activity. Dysfunctional movement patterns and faulty posture can lead to physical complaints and potential injuries, and can inhibit physical improvement. Without learning to concentrate it is impossible to change dysfunctional patterns.

the mind–body link

The Pilates Method follows a holistic approach to exercise, which means that it looks at the body and mind as a whole. The entire body needs to be taken into consideration. For example, the posture of the neck cannot be corrected unless the entire posture is looked at, from the feet right up to the base of the skull. There is never a single muscle that functions incorrectly by itself. There is always a codependence of several muscles involved.

Similarly, working out without concentration can leave psychological and emotional issues untouched. You then miss out on the opportunity to heal yourself and your body by gaining awareness. Your

KEYS TO CONCENTRATION

Concentration techniques require patience and practice. It may seem unimportant and uncomplicated but it is not.

A quiet, peaceful environment is essential if you are to achieve full relaxation and focus. Avoid brightly lit or noisy rooms.

The "Imprinting" exercise detailed on pp. 28–29 is a good way to find focus if you are tense and struggling to concentrate.

emotional and psychological experiences are reflected in your body and your behavior. Your body tends to contract when you are anxious and to open and expand when you are happy. You only have to think of a frightened child curled up in bed, or a successful athlete leaping for joy, to see the link between emotional and physical expression.

We store emotional experiences both mentally and physically. If any of these experiences have had a strong impact, we can adapt a "physical habit" in order to cope with the situation. Over time, these habits become dysfunctional and stand in the way of further physical improvement. If severe, they can even cause discomfort and injury.

movement and holding patterns

Another example of personal experiences having a physical legacy is in our reflex to pain, which can lead to "compensatory movement patterns" and "holding patterns." People sometimes adopt these patterns in order to avoid pain. In the case of long-term (chronic) injuries, these compensatory patterns can easily turn into unconscious habits. Sometimes the adapted physical behavior can itself lead to injury. This shows how it is only through the awareness that comes from concentration that you can make true physical improvements.

pilates and meditation

There is another reason why concentration is one of the six Pilates principles. In order to augment the effects of our activities and economize on effort, it is necessary to learn to focus and relax the mind. Life in the 21st century is pressurized, hectic, and noisy. We live at such a fast pace nowadays that we have trouble concentrating on any one thing at a time. Most of us hunger for peace, quiet, and relaxation. Practicing Pilates can be seen as a form of meditation, by which one uses physical exercise to calm the mind.

Learning to concentrate is essential in order to achieve the full benefit of physical exercise.

principle 2: concentration cont.

relaxation and focus

The following exercise—called "imprinting"— is an exploration technique devised by Eve Gentry, a student of Joseph Pilates. The exercise aims to release the spine and, at the same time, bring the energy down into the physical center (or inner unit) of the body. Gentry recognized the need to acquire relaxation and softness in order to gain focus, strength, and concentration. She

EXERCISE: IMPRINTING

1 To start, lie on your back with your knees bent and your feet and knees in line with your hips.

2 Calmly inhale through your nose and exhale through your mouth, following the rhythm of the breath and the rise and fall of the abdominals. The imprinting starts at the base of the skull, at the point of the highest vertebra (the atlas).

3 On the inhale, think of expanding with air— front, back, and sideways.

4 On the exhale, allow the atlas vertebra to weigh down toward the floor, as if it is making an imprint in the surface you are lying on.

tool to achieve these goals and incorporated the technique into many Pilates-related exercises. As a result, her technique has had a great influence on the remedial side of the Method.

THE BENEFIT OF IMPRINTING

This exercise takes up quite a bit of time and is not always needed in every Pilates workout. However, it is a handy exercise to use if your body and mind are full of tension and you cannot find a state of focus and concentration. It is also a useful relaxation exercise when you want to release tight back muscles and tension in the spine.

5 On the next inhale, gently breathe into that imprint while addressing the next vertebra down. Trace the individual vertebrae down, one by one until you reach the lowest ones—the sacrum and tailbones (coccyx). At this point you should feel your back lengthened and widened on the floor and the front of the body resting supportively toward the back. The front of the body softens into the spine.

6 To challenge the stability of the lower back, stretch one leg along the floor and then the other leg. While you do this, there should be no movement in the lower back or pelvis.

7 Now draw each leg back, one after the other, returning to the starting position.

8 Now start rocking your pelvis forward and back, following the rhythm of your breath. This warms the lower spine in readiness for the program (see pp. 50–91).

principle 3: center

In the Pilates Method, we always aim to move from a stable physical center. All exercises stabilize and mobilize at the same time. Without a stable physical center, movement becomes chaotic and unclear and may even cause damage to your body. There are many ways in which one can approach the physical center. Pilates, as it stands today, has a different understanding of this than the way Joseph Pilates saw it.

As time moves on, knowledge evolves and so has the Pilates Method. In particular, our understanding of the "biomechanics" of the body has changed. We now have much more accurate knowledge of anatomy than was available at the time the Method was first developed. However, the importance of having a strong physical center is still a key principle.

Joseph Pilates understood the importance of using the abdominal muscles to stabilize the lower back. He recognized that the lower back is vulnerable and exposed when not supported in movement. His description of the center of the body was as the "power house," with the navel at its center. In any lying down (supine) exercise he would ask the

INCORRECT POSTURE

STABILIZING CENTER

In order to stabilize the lower back, it is of prime importance to control the placement of the pelvis and rib cage in relation to the lumbar spine. In movement you can perform centralized activities, but you can also move off center. Your sense of physical center may change in relation to the direction and gravitational pull of your movement. However, the center of your pelvis should always be the base of your movement. Muscle movements that pull in opposite directions will stabilize the center point.

In most Pilates exercises, one part of the body stabilizes while another moves. There are a few exercises such as "Rolling Like a Ball," the "Open Leg Rocker," and the "Swan Dive," where the point of stabilization is to be found within the body while the body is constantly moving through space.

client to press the lower spine into the mat and draw the navel toward the spine.

a stable center

These days, we understand that there is no need to press the spine into the mat and that, in fact, you do not necessarily want to "flatten out" your back. The spine has various natural curvatures and it is not necessarily anatomically correct to flatten any of them. The concept of the "neutral spine" is a central concept in Pilates (see p. 49).

However, it is important to find deep abdominal and core strength to support the lumbar spine. Rather than seeing the navel as the center of the power house, we need to search deeper and lower down into the pelvis and connect the deeper abdominals and the pelvic floor at the same time. A stable center is not just found through muscular effort. The postural relation between rib cage, lumbar spine, and pelvis is crucial. One can greatly increase the downward curvature (lordosis) of the lumbar spine by simply thrusting the rib cage—or tilting the pelvis—forward.

INCORRECT POSTURE   CORRECT POSTURE

EXERCISE: FINDING CENTER-POINT OF CENTER

1	Sit comfortably and upright. Inhale, and then exhale deeply and slowly through your mouth.
2	Imagine an egg placed right in the middle of your pelvis. On exhalation, gently draw your sitting bones together and pull your pelvic floor up toward this "egg." Slowly gather the front of the pelvis and gently draw the base of the ribs down toward the pelvis so that the center point gets elevated inside the pelvis. At the same time, try to maintain optimum elongation in the lower back and both waistlines.
3	Maintain the feeling of "pull-up" that this abdominal contraction has brought about and take the next inhalation laterally, expanding the kidney area and the floating ribs as if you were breathing through gills in the middle of your back.

principle 4: precision

This principle goes hand-in-hand with placement, but does not mean quite the same thing. It is important to try to execute Pilates exercises as precisely as possible. Each exercise has a very specific goal and the goal will be missed if any of the exercise details are skipped. Of course, just how many details can be encompassed at one time depends on the capacity of the individual, but the effort of trying and concentrating will determine the eventual success of the exercise.

On an anatomical level, correct placement is crucial. Any exercise in Pilates is targeted toward a particular set of muscles. Muscles move the bones and so are dependent on the way the bones are arranged—their "spatial relationship." Correct skeletal placement and concentration are two very important keys to the correct and desired muscle recruitment. Within this principle lies another: in order to have freedom of movement, you have to stabilize internally. In other words: you keep one bone still, using "deep stabilizers," in order to mobilize another with "movers."

Replicating the movements of an exercise may look simple, but it is the detail that is important. Appearance is always secondary to the precise movements and goal of the exercise in Pilates.

the concept of isolation

This brings us to "Isolation." Let's take a movement like a golf swing as an example to illustrate this idea. A golfer needs to hit the ball in such a way that the ball ends up falling at exactly the right spot. The entire body needs to move and support the swing in order to achieve this aim. The action of the swing itself comes from the arms and shoulder joints. This is supported by the movement of the rest of the body. From the feet, through the pelvis, spine, shoulder girdle, and arm, there is a spiraling activity, serving and supporting the direction of the swing. In the action of the arms and shoulder joints it is fundamental that the shoulder blades remain placed and stable in order to let the arm swing freely and purposefully. If the shoulder blade moves with the arm, the swing will be less precise and less successful.

By practicing precision, correct placement and muscle recruitment, pure concentration, and the correct use of the breath to support an action, Pilates can support any activity, whether day-to-day or sport-linked. It will improve physical skill and capacity by promoting correct anatomical functioning. However, precision is not just about the activity of the musculoskeletal system itself. It is also concerned with the quality and control of the individual movements. This brings us to the last two Pilates principles.

PRINCIPLES OF PRECISION

1	It is essential to understand the specific goal and details of a particular exercise. Concentration is a vital component of this principle.
2	Isolating particular body parts and movements is vital. Try to concentrate on as many details of the exercise as you can while maintaining stability.
3	By taking time and care to study your anatomical functioning you will improve your movement in everyday life.

principle 5: flow

Flow can be interpreted in many different ways and we will now explore some of these. One interpretation of "flow" could be a picture of on-going, soft, and gentle movement. But this is not necessarily what is meant by "flow" in Pilates. Flow can have many different qualities. There is "bound flow," like a horse pulling a carriage up a mountain, or "free flow," like a free-flowing river. There are different "flowing rhythms," such as andante, staccato, waltz, and

The temptation to hold your breath when holding a position must be resisted if you are to enjoy the benefits of the exercise.

mazurka. Each of these has its own individual rhythmic flow.

stagnated energy

One can have different movement qualities and different movement rhythms. However, the crucial point is that both movement and breath must keep flowing. The flow of movement and breath is physiologically vital in order to keep oxygen flowing through the body, to the brain, organs, and muscles. Stagnated energy, and holding a movement and your breath, causes a build-up of lactic acid in the muscles, and this leads to tension, tightness, and subsequent discomfort. This does not mean that you cannot hold a position,

but while holding you should remain in control, without creating tension—and, above all, you must keep breathing.

There is another very important aspect to Flow that is necessary for structural fitness. Flowing movement keeps the joints healthy and mobile as well as promoting muscle balance. Dysfunctional movement patterns always indicate a disruption in the flow of movement. By simply moving and promoting flow you can gradually dissolve dysfunctional movement patterns. In fact, movement itself

EXERCISE: AROUND THE WORLD—VERSION ONE

1 Lie on your side with both knees bent toward your chest and both arms out to the side, just below shoulder height.

2 Start drawing a large circle around your head with one arm while following your fingertips with your eyes. As your arm passes over your head to the other side of your body, allow your head to turn with it. Complete the circle and bring your arm to come back to its starting position.

3 It is important to keep gravity in the arm and yet have a sense of energy and length through the fingertips. Take care not to lift your head off the floor—just let it roll and follow the fingertips. Your aim is to make the circle as smooth and easy as possible, without any disruption.

4 Each time, you will notice that your circle widens a little more, easing muscles and tendons. Circle two to four times in each direction on both sides. If you do not feel any benefit from this exercise, move on to Version Two (see p. 36).

principle 5: flow cont.

can be the cure for movement dysfunction, no matter how small and tiny these movements are.

This does not apply to inflammatory conditions, which require rest to allow healing. However, dysfunctional movement needs exercise to regain flow and coordination. One of the best examples of this type of dysfunctional movement is the inability to complete a circle with the arm. If the circle is limited and disrupted, there is muscle imbalance and limited joint mobility. Optimum joint mobility, of course, depends on the age and structure of the individual.

It is equally important to maintain a healthy muscle balance so that you do not lose any movement skills and physical strength, and to avoid unnecessary build-up of tightness.

For example, frozen-shoulder injuries are the cause of muscle imbalance problems that initially cause movement dysfunction and can steadily worsen until eventually there is no movement at all.

The following two exercises are examples that highlight and promote the principle of Flow. One exercise is for the shoulder. The other promotes a sequential rolling through the spine, which is one of the fundamental physical aims of Pilates. Sequential rolling and moving through the spine promotes good articulation and flexibility of the spine, and ensures the muscle pairs closest to the spine are strengthened equally.

EXERCISE: AROUND THE WORLD—VERSION TWO

This second version provides a deeper stretch and takes the exercise a little further. It is not suitable for a painful neck or lower back, unless performed under expert supervision.	**2**	Bend your right knee in toward your chest and place your left arm on the outside of the right knee. Take the right knee over to the left and keep reaching the left hand in opposition, looking at the fingertips of your left hand. You can let the left leg leave the floor a little, but not if the position causes neck pain.
1	To start, lie on your back with your legs long and your arms stretched out to either side of your body.	**3**	Now draw the same arm circle as in Version One. Again, try to follow your fingertips with your eyes. If the movement jumps in certain places, stay there and simply breathe in and out in order to ease the tightness in the shoulder before moving on.

EXERCISE: SLOW ROLL DOWN THROUGH THE SPINE

This exercise seems very slow and simple but is actually surprisingly difficult. It highlights "blind" spots in the spine, particularly of the lumbar spine, and any corresponding weakness in the neighboring abdominal muscles. The first sacral vertebra referred to is in your lower back, in line with your pelvis, where the inward curvature of the lower spine begins.

1 Sit upright with your knees bent up and your feet on the floor in line with your hips. Place your hands behind your knees and very slowly and gradually roll the spine down into the mat. On the exhale, curl the first sacral vertebra down.

2 Inhale, hold the position, and then exhale. On the exhale, roll the next two vertebrae down and again inhale and hold the position.

3 Very slowly lower your body a little bit further each time, moving your hands down the back of the spine for support. Make sure you roll through each junction of the spine: first, the junction between the sacrum and the lumbar spine (where the upward inner-curvature starts) and second, the junction between the lumbar and thoracic spine (where the inner-curvature ends). Try to avoid giving in to gravity and falling back down to the floor.

4 Once you are all the way down on the floor, allow your knees to fall to one side and then come back to the sitting position. Repeat the exercise two or three times and notice how your abdominals soften and yet start working deeper, and how you roll more easily through the spine.

principle 6: control

Control is the last of Pilates' original principles. The word "control" can have a negative connotation, reflecting obsession and limitation. This is not what is meant by "Control" in Pilates. Here, the aim is to achieve control of mind and body, and of movement and breathing. Initially, the Pilates Method was called "The Art of Contrology." Pilates wrote two books on the subject in which he explained the principles and thoughts behind his Method.

His ultimate aim was to achieve total control of one's body and of one's movement. Pilates believed that you can stay fit and healthy and fight sickness and disease by maintaining the right attitude and by following the right exercise. He also saw the value of exercise as a way to

ADDITIONAL PRINCIPLES

There are many principles we could add to the original list of six to expand our understanding of the Pilates Method. The three additional ones listed here are the most important. They were added by Fran Lehen, a veteran Pilates teacher from New York, who ran the Groundfloor Studio in Manhattan.

COORDINATION

Coordination is relative and depends on the individual, but is a very important point to consider. Athletes need to be as skilled and coordinated as possible in their chosen sport. A dancer needs to coordinate movement with music. For the ordinary person, coordination may seem much less relevant, yet it is just as important.

We all need to practice coordination as a skill. Non-coordinated movement brings about disrupted movement patterns, faulty placement, and possibly incorrect muscle recruitment. This leads to minor injuries, inhibits physical improvement, and may result in the loss of physical skills. One example of this is where an elderly person gradually loses mobility and coordination and ends up moving very little. In this case, lack of agility means the smallest incident can lead to injury. Therefore, it is always useful to practice coordination and keep improving movement skills.

Pilates teaches coordination of movement and breath. Once movement and breath are integrated you can add further stages as a challenge, such as including arm, leg, and head movements.

keep up your spirits in times of depression and despair.

When interned in England during World War I, Pilates taught his fellow internees a range of exercises that were designed to keep them healthy and to help them develop a positive mental attitude during their captivity. These exercises were designed for a confined space and were to become the system we now know as the Pilates Method.

Pilates' attitude to life could be summed up as "mind over matter," and this positive outlook led him to view exercise as a link between body and mind. A Pilates student learns to control body and movement by integrative Method to gain an awareness and skill that can be integrated into daily life and other physical and sporting activities.

RELAXATION

The Pilates Method involves exercise with relaxed control. Working correctly promotes the most efficient use of muscular effort. Using your muscles in a functional and efficient way creates the least amount of tension. The fact that this Method is supported by the correct use of breath, focus, and concentration, all helps to rid the mind of unnecessary thoughts and therefore acts as a form of meditation.

Relaxation is a principle that can be acquired through the right amount of effort to achieve your goals. Pilates exercises fail in their effect if they are performed with too much effort or when carried out under pressure. The more you gain inner strength, the more relaxed you become, and the more able you are to execute the most difficult exercises. Of course, the latter does not happen overnight. Building up deep inner strength and undoing unwanted tension requires concentration and regular practice. If Pilates feels like a chore that creates tension, the Method has little chance of being effective. It should be enjoyable to learn and leave you feeling rejuvenated.

STAMINA

Joseph Pilates originally devised his Method as a physical workout. Nowadays, the Pilates Method has gained a reputation as a great form of treatment, and many of the exercises have been adapted for remedial purposes. However, the remedial side is only one aspect of the work. In essence, Pilates should always aim to challenge the client further—within reason—and no client should end up following the same program for years on end. The body becomes lazy if it is not challenged and pushed into the area of the "unknown." It is up to the Pilates teacher to remain alert to the need to deepen the client's body awareness and physical skills further, when ready, and to provide appropriate variations and a new repertoire, when desired. This is the stamina you should be working toward when studying Pilates.

The Pilates Method does not directly address cardiovascular, or aerobic, stamina—a form of stamina that is another very important factor in any exercise regime that promotes health. However, because it focuses on breathing and anatomical efficiency, Pilates does *support* all forms of cardiovascular activity and may even improve them.

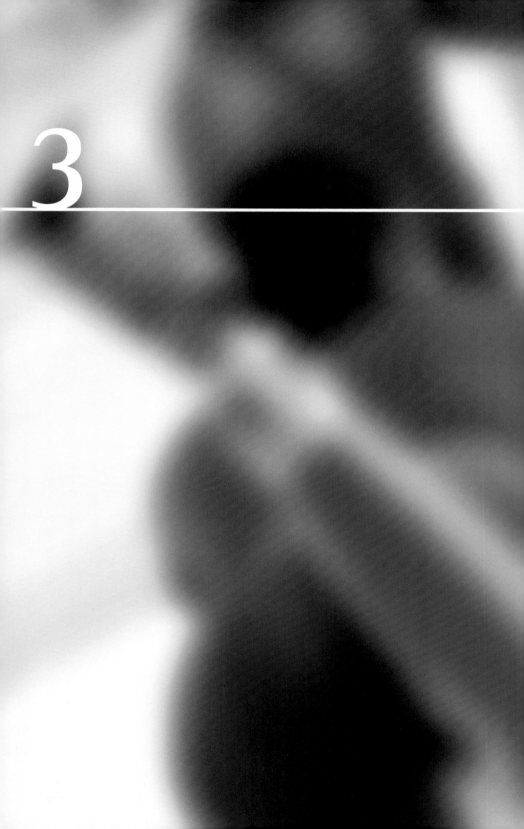

3

physical fundamentals

There are a number of fundamental principles that you need to be aware of when practicing Pilates. The body is a marvelously complex structure that is subject to many different pressures as you journey through life. Gravity, age, occupation, and nutrition are only a few of the external and internal forces that affect your musculoskeletal system and hence your physical well-being. This, in turn, means your body requires more thoughtful, or "mindful," input to perform at its optimal level. This chapter explores all the fundamental principles that affect your body.

the right focus

Exercising your musculoskeletal system has an effect on the bones, joints, blood supply, and internal organs—as well as on the connective tissue that joins them all together. If you can develop an understanding of how the major muscle groups work, you can choose the appropriate exercises to improve your physical structure.

Attempting to exercise without a knowledge of basic anatomy in general, and your own physical structure in particular, is like trying to run uphill with very heavy ankle weights on. You'll be wasting effort and energy that could be put to better use in helping you to achieve your aims. Joseph Pilates understood this. Therefore his method of exercising is based on certain key concepts that help the practitioner get the most out of the movements in the program.

posture and spine alignment

One of the main objectives of a Pilates program of exercise is to improve posture and correct any significant imbalances in the alignment of the body. Bad posture can lead to certain muscle groups being overused at the expense of others. This results in dysfunctional patterns of movement. Often a person may complain of a pain in the lower back that is almost entirely due to standing incorrectly and not using the right muscle groups to support his or her body weight. Correcting this bad posture can help to alleviate the pain and establish a new, healthier way of standing that will benefit the whole structure.

Essentially, the vertebral column acts as the central support structure for the whole body. It connects the skull to the pelvis and supports the musculature. Crucially, it also houses and protects the central nervous system (CNS)—the brain and spinal cord—and the autonomic nervous system (ANS)—which controls automatic processes such as breathing, heartbeat, and digestion.

Therefore, the well-being of this important nerve tissue is dependent on the well-being of the spine. The spine is made up of 33 vertebrae, plus the intervertebral disks that keep them apart, and all the cartilaginous structures (ligaments, bands of cartilage,

PILATES FUNDAMENTALS

The following fundamentals, which are not exhaustive, highlight the anatomical principles upon which Pilates is based:

1	Posture and alignment of the spine
2	Position of the head and neck
3	Weight-bearing tripod of the feet
4	Pelvic and shoulder girdle alignment
5	The concept of the neutral spine

and connective tissue) that link the bones and help to hold them together.

When you are young, these structures are highly resilient—even a "slipping" intervertebral disk can return to its correct position so that it can continue to do its job and function well. But, as we age, not only do the forces of gravity and life press ever more heavily upon us (physically and psychologically) but these structures become less resilient and less able to cope with traumatic shocks or extreme muscular effort.

The intervertebral disks grow thin and may get squeezed out of shape (herniated) or even split, and the bones grow less dense, becoming more brittle—in short these structures become more vulnerable. Posture is not only affected by such changes but is also an important factor in preventing deterioration.

If the spine is held in the most beneficial position for facilitating movement and distributing weight, the body is able to withstand the pressures of gravity and aging most effectively. The muscles are then able to work together correctly, each doing its proper job, and imbalance and strain will be banished.

You will need a full-length mirror in order to evaluate your own posture and alignment. You can then look at every aspect of your stance from the front and from both sides. If you are lucky enough to have two large mirrors that you can place facing one another, you can even see yourself from the back. If not, ask a friend to hold a mirror behind you.

Evaluate your own posture in a full-length mirror, examining every aspect of your stance from the front and both sides.

look at yourself

Facing the mirror, take a look at your general stance and see whether you can spot any areas of tension and imbalance.

1 Do your shoulders look hunched?

2 Is one shoulder higher than the other? (Ask yourself how often you take a call with the phone scrunched between your shoulder and your neck!)

3 Do you have a sway back, or bow legs?

4 Is one hip higher than the other and/or rotated forward or back?

5 Do you seem to have your weight forward on your toes, or back on your heels?

In an ideal stance, you should look as though you might be able to hang a hypothetical weighted line from the crown of your head to a point directly between the ankles. The front, back, and sides of the body should be equally aligned on either side of the weighted line. When this is the case, the weight of the body is evenly distributed through all the joints. If your alignment is "off center," some joints will carry more weight than others and so be more prone to wear and tear.

Now look at yourself from the side and study your spine.

6 Is your lower back arched?

7 Is your upper back curved too far forward?

8 Does your chest stick out too much (in a "military" stance)?

9 Does your head thrust forward?

10 Is your head retracted?

11 Does your head tilt more to one side than the other?

12 Where is your weight placed in relation to your feet?

Now look for muscular imbalances. The following are all indications of imbalance and show you where you have been overdeveloping some muscle groups while leaving others weaker.

13 Do your thighs appear to be bulky in relation to the rest of you?

14 Are the muscles of the calves symmetrical, or is one lower leg larger than the other?

When viewed from the front or the back, a properly aligned spine should appear to be symmetrical. That hypothetical weighted line should "pass" through the center of the head, chest, abdomen, and buttocks. The shoulders, shoulder blades, and hips are level on the horizontal plane, unless there is a structural deviation, such as a leg-length difference or curvature of the spine.

The spine has four natural curves, or lordosis: the inward neck (cervical) curve, the outward chest (thoracic) curve, the inward lower (lumbar) curve, and the lowest (sacral) curve. These curves are formed by the shape of the vertebrae and the intervertebral disks. Correct alignment requires the maintenance of the integrity of this curved architecture. In some people, the shape of the spine does deviate from these curves: the two most common deviations being a sideways S-shaped curve (scoliosis) and an exaggeration of the thoracic curve or "hunchback" (khyphosis).

In a scoliotic spine, the muscles on either side of the spine are noticeably under-developed on one side but bulging, or overdeveloped, on the other. In a kyphotic spine, the muscles of the upper torso are overdeveloped, the shoulders are hunched and rounded forward, and the neck muscles are contracted, causing the head to jut forward.

Pilates is extremely beneficial for improving the posture of anyone suffering from these conditions (which may be structural, or caused by bad posture or repetitious movements owing to an individual's occupation). The exercises work to strengthen weak muscles and to stretch out tight, bunched areas, and thus realign the musculature and its support structure.

position of the head and neck

The position of the head and neck are dependent on the posture of the spine as a whole. An exaggerated thoracic curve, for example, leads to a rounded upper back, tight shoulders, and a head position that is thrust forward. The neck muscles are tight and the shoulder muscles bunched. Head movement is restricted and the head will tilt back in an uncomfortable position when the individual is lying flat.

In this case a cushion needs to be placed under the head to bring the head back into correct alignment with the rest of the spine. Sometimes the muscles on one side of the neck become tighter than those on the other side and the head is pulled over to one side, or the muscles at the front of the neck become shortened, causing the head to appear retracted.

There are various exercises that can be used to remedy problems of this kind. The simplest method involves stretching the major neck muscles in a full range of directions (forward, back, side-to-side,

EXERCISES: HEAD-TO-KNEE STRETCH

1 Sitting upright, tilt your head to one side and then look at one knee. Place a hand over the side of the skull and gently draw the head down toward that knee. Hold for a count of five, feeling the stretch. Then release and repeat on the other side.

2 Place your hands behind your head. Inhale and draw your elbows together. Exhale and roll your head forward until you feel your neck muscles have stretched as far as is comfortable. Take care not to pull on your neck. Raise and lower your head six times.

and rotation) in order to lengthen the tight muscles, while creating resistance within these stretches that simultaneously strengthens weak areas. As all muscle groups work in pairs (one being responsible for contraction and the "partner" muscle bringing about extension), it is essential to exercise them in a way that ensures the members of each pair are given equal attention regarding strength and stretching movements.

EXERCISES: CORRECTING TIGHT NECK MUSCLES

An overstretched muscle is as weak as one that is too tight. The following exercises are designed to help correct tight neck muscles that are holding the head in an incorrect position. They were devised by Eve Gentry and are invaluable for releasing painful neck and shoulder "holding" patterns.

1 Lie on your back with your knees bent, head resting on a telephone directory (or similar-sized book).

2 Imagine an orange just above your nose, and circle the orange with your nose 10 times. Now repeat in the opposite direction. Try to keep the neck long and relaxed and the circle smooth.

3 Describe a figure eight with your nose. Imagine the eight is lying on its side—like a ribbon tied in a bow. Repeat in both directions.

4 Press your chin down into your neck and your head into the book. Hold for a count of five as you exhale, feeling the neck muscles stretching out. Repeat 10 times.

5 Roll your head from side to side, slowly, feeling the full range of movement.

weight-bearing tripod of the feet

Although this is referred to as a "tripod," there are really four weight-bearing points on the feet. When standing, the main weight of the body should be divided over the four points, which together form a squared-off triangle. These points are the big-toe joint, the little-toe joint, and two points on either side of the heel. The main weight of the body should fall through the center of the feet, at the crossing of the medial and transverse arch, straight through the bone marrow.

Proper placement allows the muscles of the foot and ankle to work efficiently. If the weight is incorrectly distributed, even a tiny deviation can place a lot of stress on these joints. The ligaments that hold the bones together can become permanently stretched if they are continually pressured by faulty alignment.

The arch of the foot (formed from the metatarsal bones) is often weak (a condition sometimes described as "dropped" or "fallen" arches), which means that the main postural support for the body is inefficient. As a consequence, knees and ankles can roll in or out, causing alignment problems throughout the legs, hips, and back. Strengthening the feet and ankles can improve posture significantly and relieve pain in the hip, knee, and ankle joints.

PELVIC AND SHOULDER GIRDLE ALIGNMENT

Most back problems start either in the shoulder or the pelvic regions and are caused by instability in these two areas. Therefore, learning how to maintain the stability of the shoulders and pelvis is extremely important and is central to all Pilates work.

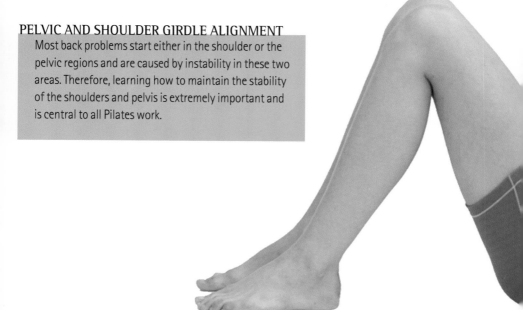

THE CONCEPT OF A NEUTRAL SPINE

1 This concept goes hand-in-hand with understanding how to place the pelvis and shoulders in correct alignment. It is a crucial concept in the Pilates philosophy.

2 In a perfect standing posture, the natural curves of the spine are equally divided on either side of the vertical weighted line.

3 When lying down, the weight-bearing points of the torso are: the back of the head, the shoulder girdle, the rib cage, and the sacrum.

4 The cervical and lumbar spine might be touching the floor, but they are essentially non-weight-bearing. The degree of curvature in the lower back varies between individuals, to some extent, but the angle between the bottom of the lumbar region and the top of the sacral region is more or less the same. This applies equally to the angle between the thoracic and lumbar regions.

5 To achieve a neutral pelvic alignment, your hipbones and pubic bone should form a horizontal triangle. In other words, you should be able to place a cup of tea between your hipbones and pubic bone and not spill it.

6 The curve in your lumbar spine is also affected by the placement of the rib cage, so your rib cage needs to relax toward your back and "open out" in order to stabilize the middle of your back.

7 If you have a hunched posture, or an exaggerated curve in the upper or lower spine, this indicates shoulder and pelvic girdle dysfunction. You should spend some time trying to achieve a neutral spinal position, as described above, before attempting to exercise.

4

the program

The exercise sequence described and illustrated in this chapter is made up of a selection of original Pilates mat exercises plus some of the more recently evolved repertoire and related exercises. The classical Pilates matwork, some film footage, and a few pieces of writing are the only legacy Joseph Pilates left. A dozen of his students, who were his apprentices and subsequently became his fellow teachers, developed and evolved the method by delving deeper into the study of the Pilates principles and fundamentals and adapting or varying the method to different needs. It is difficult, however, to call an exercise program "Pilates" if it does not contain a number of Joseph's original exercises, which can be found here.

starting your practice

If you've never tried Pilates before, explore Getting Started (pp. 6–13) and The Six Pilates Principles (pp. 14–39) first and practice some of the basic exercises before you tackle the program. They'll help you get started and remind you of the movement quality you're looking for. Your breath should conduct the rhythm of each exercise, so try to put into practice the breathing exercises described on pp. 14–39.

The step-by-step program given below is divided into four sequences:

steps and illustrations

The program is designed for beginners, so you should find that most of the exercises are reasonably easy to do. However, spinal structure and the stability and movement range of the individual joints vary from person to person. Therefore, depending on your physical makeup, level of fitness, and exercise and movement background, you may find some exercises more difficult. Attention to detail, the quality of the movement, and alignment are all

SEQUENCE 1

Introduces you to basic matwork, helping you to really get in touch with your body and, in particular, to explore the wide range of movement your spine is capable of. In this sequence, and in the following one, most of the trunk and body weight are supported by the floor.

SEQUENCE 3

Addresses posture, balance, and flexibility in different directions, or "spatial planes." We are primarily "vertical beings" who must maintain balance on our two feet, so our posture needs to be built from the base upward. Therefore it is vital to challenge balance and support in different spatial planes if we are going to relate the Pilates method to daily life.

SEQUENCE 2

Focuses on "strengthening the inner unit"— the core stabilizers that play such a vital part in healthy and efficient movement.

SEQUENCE 4

Comprises a short set of "unwinding" exercises designed to cool you down, relax your body, and prepare you for normal activities.

crucial in achieving the desired effect.

practice makes perfect

To make the most of this program, we recommend that you practice regularly, and also try to apply elements of the program to your daily life. By "regular practice" we mean at least once a week. Ideally, you should exercise every day.

If your day allows little time to perform the whole program, you can select a few exercises from each of the four parts of the program. One of the great things about learning a program like this is that you can continue to work out even when you are away on business or on vacation, and you have nothing available to exercise with but the floor and your body. The program also provides an ideal warm-up for sports, or any other physical activity you are planning.

go with the flow

Where appropriate, the text explains the best way to move from one exercise to the next. These connecting exercises, or "transitions," promote concentration and flow by enabling you to move in a clear and structured way. Once you've worked on the individual exercises, and feel you understand the mechanics, start performing them in sequence, making the transitions from one exercise to the next.

These transitions should become as important as the exercises themselves, because in the end you should aim to perform the whole program as one flowing sequence. In this way, you not

WARNING:

If you are pregnant, or suffering some form of injury, you should seek the advice of a qualified Pilates teacher before attempting these exercises. This program is not suitable for treating specific back disorders, nor for guiding women through pregnancy.

only maintain concentration but also ensure that your body remains warm, which makes aches, pain, and injury less likely. Never rush the exercises. Always keep a calm and alert mind and concentrate on the flow of your breath.

Once you know the exercises reasonably well, the total program should take you no more then 40 minutes to complete. Performed in this flowing, concentrated way, Pilates can also be a form of meditation that will clear your mind, and awaken your body.

Some people find it difficult to learn exercises and to remember to carry them out in a specific order. Don't worry if this is so in your case.
It doesn't mean that you've failed to gain the benefits of Pilates from this particular program. We all have different talents, and physical and movement memory is not always one of them. Memorizing the program in a flowing sequence is only an aid to being able to practice the exercises regularly without having to make too much effort. This makes the program more challenging and also more fun!

standing roll down

S tanding Roll Down tests your flexibility and highlights areas of tightness in your body. It also helps prepare you for the exercises that follow by getting you into the correctly aligned posture and putting you in the right frame of mind.

STANDING ROLL DOWN—ALL LEVELS

1

Stand with your feet in line with your hips, head facing forward.

Check that your weight falls slightly forward over the balls of your feet, but is distributed throughout the weight-bearing tripod of the feet (see p. 48). Keep your abdominal muscles drawn in.

Inhaling, roll your chin down toward your chest and then start to exhale as you roll the rest of your spine smoothly forward toward the floor.

how's it going?

As you do this exercise, note any areas of tension, or tightness, in your body. For example, the hamstrings (at the back of the thigh) may feel tight, or the lower back, neck, or shoulders may be stiff as you roll down. Also try to remember to keep your weight evenly distributed between both feet and try not to lean back as you roll forward. This is a common error—your body will try to compensate for moving your weight forward by leaning back.

⏶how's it going?

Draw your navel toward your spine so that the abdominal muscles support the movement and try not to lock, or "sway back," the knees.

Once you have rolled as far as is comfortable, inhale into your back and then exhale as you roll back up to your original standing position. Repeat two to three times.

To move into the Seated Ripple from the position above, slightly flex your knees and bend one knee at a time onto the floor until you are on all fours. From here, sit back on your heels, move your pelvis and feet to one side, and swing both legs in front of you until you can sit up straight with your knees bent up.

▶▶

1

seated ripple

The Seated Ripple encourages you to articulate your entire spine in flexion and to open the upper back and chest in extension. The emphasis is on the movement—not on muscular effort.

SEATED RIPPLE—ALL LEVELS

2

Sit up as tall as you can with your knees bent and your feet on the floor. Place your hands on the front of your knees, fingers pointing

toward each other. Make sure your elbows are open and your shoulder blades are down and wide across your back. Inhale.

As you exhale, feel your abdominals softening and scooping toward the spine. Curl first the tailbone and then the rest of the pelvis under you.

On the next inhalation (through your nose), imagine your spine filling up with air from the bottom to the top and opening up wide across the back.

Still inhaling, bring the pelvis, then the lower, middle, and upper back, and finally the neck and head, vertical. Think of building the spine like a stack of blocks.

On the last inhalation, pull your hands against your knees and open your chest up to the ceiling, arching your upper back while keeping your neck long and in line with the spine.

how's it going?

When doing this exercise, it is useful to think of the back of the torso as being divided into five parts: pelvis, lower back, middle back, upper back, and neck and head. Also, this exercise is a comfortable warm-up for the spine and is ideal for opening up the chest. The Seated Ripple can also be performed seated on a stool or chair, with your hands placed firmly on your thighs. Your hands should push gently away when flexing and gently toward you when arching. Watch that you do not overarch your lower back; the aim is just to open your chest.

⬆how's it going?

Follow with the lower back, middle back, upper back, and finally your head and neck.

Pay attention to articulating each junction from one part of the spine to the next.

This will take you into a deep "C-curve." All the air is now out of your lungs.

On a suspended breath, bring your head and neck back to the vertical. The ripple can then start again from the top. Repeat four to six times.

To move into the Pelvic Tilt from the last position shown above, place your hands behind your knees and slowly walk your hands up the back of your thighs toward your pelvis, while very slowly

rolling the spine, vertebra by vertebra, down onto the floor, until you are lying on your back.

▸▸

1

pelvic tilt & shoulder bridge preparation

Both the Pelvic Tilt and Shoulder Bridge Preparation aim to flex and articulate the spine and stabilize the pelvis. Both exercises strengthen the abdominals, gluteals, and hamstrings.

PELVIC TILT—ALL LEVELS

3

You should now be lying on the floor with your knees bent and your feet flat on the floor. Make sure your feet and knees are in line with your hips, your arms are by your side, and your head and neck are relaxed.

Exhale to allow your abdomen to soften toward your spine and then inhale into your back and sides. Then exhale as you scoop your pelvic floor and abdomen deeply in toward your spine and peel your tailbone, pelvis, middle, and lower back off the floor.

Aim to articulate each individual vertebra, while keeping the pelvis level and the neck long, until you have created one long diagonal line from your breastbone to your knees.

SHOULDER BRIDGE PREPARATION—BEGINNER TO INTERMEDIATE LEV

4

Start in a full Pelvic Tilt (see above) and hold the pelvis in a flexed position at the same height from the floor throughout. Make sure your hips are even.

Inhale and bend your left knee up to the ceiling, taking your weight onto the right leg. Watch that the left hip does not drop down, and keep the right foot firmly planted on the weight-bearing tripod of the feet (see p. 48).

Exhale, and extend the back of your left leg so that your foot points up to the ceiling. Keep your torso and supporting leg completely still.

how's it going?

If you want a greater challenge, follow the Pelvic Tilt with the Shoulder Bridge Preparation. Otherwise, move on to Abdominal Curls. The Shoulder Bridge Preparation is very useful for balancing pelvic instability, and stabilizing the body with one leg requires good toning in the hamstrings and the buttock muscles (in particular, the *gluteus medius* and *minimus*).

⬆how's it going?

Inhale into your back and sides while keeping your abdomen pulled in toward your spine (see pp. 24–25).

On the next exhalation, start softening the collarbone, then the breastbone, middle back, lower back, and pelvis, and finally relax your tailbone until your back is resting on the floor.

Repeat the exercise six to eight times, then either continue with the Shoulder Bridge Preparation or move on to the Abdominal Curl.

Inhale and bend the extended leg back toward the ground. On the next exhalation, place the foot back down into the Pelvic Tilt position.

Once you have completed this movement on the left leg, repeat the same action on the right leg. Repeat three to five times on each side.

Finish the exercise by sequentially rolling down through the spine to the ground as described in the Pelvic Tilt (see above).

▶▶

abdominal curl & oblique preparation

The Abdominal Curl works all four of the abdominal muscle groups and prepares them for the exercises ahead. The Oblique Preparation exercise is a simple and safe oblique exercise.

ABDOMINAL CURL—BEGINNER LEVEL

5

Lie on your back with your knees bent and your feet flat on the floor. Clasp your hands behind your head with your elbows slightly off the floor and your shoulders relaxed.

Exhale as you engage the abdominal muscles and roll your head and neck forward, supporting them with your hands. Draw your shoulder blades down so your neck stays relaxed. Your pelvis should remain in a neutral position.

Inhale and lift your right knee so your thigh is at a 90-degree angle to your body. Feel your abdominals contract as they support the lifting of the leg. Keep your neck, shoulders, and back muscles relaxed.

OBLIQUE PREPARATION—BEGINNER LEVEL

6

Follow on from the previous position, lying on your back on the floor, with your knees bent up and your feet and knees in line with your hips. Place your right hand behind your head and leave your left arm beside your body.

On exhalation, curl your head and upper body forward and up into an abdominal curl position and raise your left hand just off the floor, alongside your hip, reaching toward your feet as you do so.

On the next inhalation, twist your upper body toward the left without disturbing the neutral placement of the pelvis.

how's it going?

Take care not to force the movement of the Abdominal Curl, which might strain your neck or lower back. Try to keep your pelvis in the neutral position (see p. 49) and avoid tensing the back muscles. Oblique Preparation is safe because it does not involve holding the weight of your legs from your abdominals, as in the Criss Cross exercise (see pp. 74-75).

⬆how's it going?

Exhale as you contract your lower abdominals further, and raise your left leg. Inhale, and start to curl up, bringing your knees toward your chin and contracting your lower abdominals as much as you can.

Exhale and uncurl, rolling your upper back toward the floor and moving your knees away from you. Draw your abdominals in as tightly as possible. Do not arch your lower back as you lower your back onto the floor.

Finish where you began, with your spine relaxed back onto the floor, your pelvis in neutral, your neck long, and your hands on the floor.

As you exhale, raise your left hand up and just along the knee. Inhale and lower your arm. Repeat this action four times.

On the fourth lift of your arm, keep it up and turn your upper body and hand to the right. Do eight little pulses (short up-and-down movements) on each exhale in this position. On the next inhalation, return your body back to center and as you exhale, relax back to your starting position.

As you inhale, switch the position of your arms and repeat the exercise on the other side. Do two repetitions on each side. To move into the Roll Up, place both arms beside your body and slide your legs one by one onto the floor. Make sure that your lower back is supported by your abdominals while you do this.

▶▶

roll up & swimming

Roll Up strengthens and stretches the muscles of the back, articulates the vertebrae, and strengthens the abdominals. Swimming targets the back extensor muscles that help us to balance while standing upright.

ROLL UP—BEGINNER TO INTERMEDIATE LEVEL

7

Lie on your back with your legs extended in front of you. Place your arms behind your head, palms toward the ceiling. Holding a pole helps to keep your shoulders level and gives you something concrete to focus on as you roll up. If you don't have access to a pole, you can perform the exercise without it.

Keep your pelvis in a neutral position so that there is a small, natural arch in your lower back. Press your ankles together and flex your feet, keeping your heels on the floor. Keep your knees slightly soft so that your thighs are not gripping the floor.

Inhale as you reach your arms up and forward and roll your head toward your chest, lifting your head and shoulders off the floor. Press your inner thighs together and begin to scoop your abdominals into your center.

SWIMMING—BEGINNER TO INTERMEDIATE LEVEL

8

Lie face down with your arms by your sides and palms facing up. Think of creating length in the front of your hip sockets, stretching right through the front of your legs to your feet. Maintain this feeling throughout the exercise.

On an inhalation, extend your shoulder blades across and down your back and reach out with the fingertips.

As you continue to inhale, lengthen through the crown of your head. Gently start to lift your head, breastbone, and upper back off the floor. Make sure you keep your neck in line with the arching of your spine.

how's it going?

On the Roll Up, if you are unable to roll up without raising your shoulders, lifting your legs and feet off the floor, or tensing your back, start with your knees bent and roll up as far as you can without throwing yourself into it. Also, beginners should roll back only halfway, bending their knees. On Swimming, the lower back arches much more easily than the upper back and so tends to carry all the strain. In any back-extensor exercise, such as Swimming, aim to lengthen and support the lower back as much as possible, while emphasizing opening the upper back and chest.

⬧how's it going?

WARNING: THIS EXERCISE SHOULD NOT BE ATTEMPTED BY ANYONE WITH A DISORDER OF THE LOWER BACK. ▶▶

Begin to exhale as you peel off the floor, reaching your arms in front of you. Focus your effort on scooping the abdominal muscles in order to lift yourself up and forward into a C-shape. Keep your legs on the floor and avoid gripping with your thigh muscles to pull you up. Pause.

To reverse the movement, inhale and roll your tailbone underneath you. Then exhale for one long breath as you roll back down to your original position. Keep squeezing your abdominals in as you do so. Repeat the sequence 10 times.

To move into Swimming, from your supine position (lying on your back) roll over onto your stomach and bring your arms down by your side, palms facing the ceiling. Rest your forehead on the floor and keep your neck long.

On the next exhalation, continue traveling up while the palms of your hands rotate toward the floor.

In the same movement, move your hands out to the side so your arms make a V-shape and finally reach a parallel position beside your ears. Make sure your shoulders are relaxed and down.

Maintain an elongated form throughout the whole of the front of your body in order to support the arching of your back.

swimming (cont.) ▶▶

2

swimming & hip rolls

This is the second part of the Swimming exercise. Hip Rolls works the oblique abdominal muscles and stretches a major side flexor of the spine and spinal rotators. It also mobilizes the thoracic spine.

SWIMMING (cont.)

9

From this elongated and strongly supported position, lift both legs off the floor and reestablish an equal bow shape throughout your entire body.

Breathe in for five counts and breathe out for five counts while "swimming" the arms and legs up and down, left arm with right leg, and vice versa. Repeat for five breaths.

Finish in the elongated bow shape before lowering your legs. Maintain the length in the front of your body and through your hip sockets.

HIP ROLLS—ALL LEVELS

10

Lie on your back, as described at the end of Swimming. Inhale, then as you exhale, lift one foot off the floor. Inhale, then exhale as you lift the other foot off the floor until both knees are at a 90-degree angle to the body. Place a ball between your knees.

Exhale and twist to the left, taking your head in the opposite direction. Keep the ball between your knees in the same position throughout.

Anchor your shoulder blades to the floor and only roll over as far as you can without the shoulder you are rolling away from lifting off the floor.

how's it going?

With Swimming, once you have arrived in the final rest position, rock your hips gently and freely from side to side. This eases the vertebrae and muscles of the lower back. There are two versions of the Hip Rolls; if you find the exercise shown here too difficult, do not raise your legs but simply keep your feet on the ground until you feel strong enough to hold your legs safely parallel to the floor. In either case, try to breathe laterally into your upper back throughout the exercise. This will help keep your back relaxed.

↥how's it going?

On an exhalation, place your hands on your forehead and lower your body back down to the floor.

You can repeat this sequence two or three times, each time creating a little more length in the front of your body.

To move into Hip Rolls, roll onto your back and bend your knees up so that your feet and knees are in line with your hips, and your feet are flat on the floor. Open your arms out to the side, keeping them just below shoulder height.

WARNING: DO NOT ATTEMPT THIS EXERCISE IF YOU HAVE AN EXISTING BACK PROBLEM.

Return to center, inhaling, pressing your ribs down as before and contracting the oblique abdominals.

Repeat on the other side, twisting to the right. Keep your neck long and shoulders relaxed and maintain a neutral pelvis throughout.

To move into the Corkscrew, extend one leg and then the other until both are fully stretched out in front of you. Bring your arms down by your sides, palms into the floor.

▶▶

corkscrew & 100s (beginner)

The Corkscrew strengthens the abdominal wall and back muscles, flattens the stomach, and lengthens the hamstrings. The 100s strengthens the abdominal muscles and activates the breathing.

CORKSCREW—INTERMEDIATE LEVEL

11

Inhale and bend both knees so that your feet come off the floor. Do not arch your lower back; so keep your abdominals drawn into your spine. Exhale and extend both legs to the ceiling, directly above your hips. Your tailbone should be down, pelvis in neutral, and shoulders relaxed.

Inhale, keeping your abdominals drawn into your back, and circle your legs around as if drawing an oval shape in space with your toes. As you circle to the left, your right hip will come off the floor slightly, but your lower back should remain stable. Exhale, and reverse the circle, moving your legs in the opposite direction.

100s—BEGINNER LEVEL

12

Lie on your back with your knees bent and your feet on the floor. Stretch your arms out by your sides. Inhale as you slide your arms further forward, reaching away from your shoulders. Exhale as you roll your head forward so that your eyes focus on your navel. Keep a little space between your chin and your chest, and lengthen your neck. Draw your shoulder blades down and relax your neck.

Inhale as you lift one leg up to a 90-degree angle, with your toes softly pointed. Exhale as you lift the other leg up to the same angle, so that both legs are bent and both sets of toes are pointing forward.

how's it going?

If you are having difficulty keeping your neck in line with the rest of your spine when doing the Corkscrew, place a small cushion under the back of your head. When doing the 100s, draw your abdominals into your spine. Try to feel the weight of your back dropping into the floor, while maintaining a comfortable, neutral pelvis and lumbar spine position. Remember not to push your stomach out, but to keep it scooped in at all times. This properly supports the spine and creates a flatter stomach. If your neck aches from the effort of holding it up, place a large cushion or pillow behind your head to keep it propped forward during the exercise.

▲how's it going?

Press your arms down into the floor and keep your shoulders anchored. Try to keep your neck and shoulders relaxed. If you find that your lower back is arching off the floor, bend your knees slightly.

Do five circles in each direction, alternating each time so that you do ten circles in total, inhaling for one circle, exhaling for the reverse.

To finish, bend your knees back toward your body and place your feet on the floor again.

Raise both arms off the floor so that they are in line with your hips. Keep your back in the same position and take care not to arch your lower back.

Pump your arms up and down in a small, vigorous movement, inhaling through your nose for a count of five, and exhaling through your mouth for a count of five.

Keep drawing your abdominals in and keep the breath located in your upper back.

▶▶

2

100s (intermediate) & leg circles

Leg Circles stabilize the pelvis, mobilize the hip joints, and strengthen the core abdominal, back, and leg muscles. The intermediate-level 100s is designed to further challenge your abdominal muscles.

100s—INTERMEDIATE LEVEL

13

Start in the same position as for the beginner level. Inhale as you extend both legs to the ceiling, drawing your abdominals in deeply to support the weight of your legs.

Once both legs are extended, exhale and rotate your legs out so that your heels are placed together but your feet are turned out. Flex your feet.

Squeeze your inner thighs together so that the inner thigh (adductor) muscles and the backs of the legs are activated.

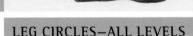

LEG CIRCLES—ALL LEVELS

14

Lie on your back, as above, arms extended alongside your body. Inhale as you lift one knee up.

Exhale and extend your leg fully to a 90-degree angle to your body. Flex the heel. Drop the hip joint down into the floor and anchor the pelvis in a neutral position. Scoop your abdominals in to support your back.

Inhale and draw a large circle in the air, taking the leg across the body first and keeping your hips on the floor. Finish the circle when your leg is back at its starting point, pointing at the ceiling.

how's it going?

Only attempt the intermediate-level 100s once you have mastered the beginner's level on the previous page. The intermediate-level 100s requires careful breathing, so keep your breathing focused and into your back so that the abdominals can work properly. The back muscles should be relaxed, especially the neck, shoulders, and lumbar regions. When performing Leg Circles, imagine your leg reaching toward the ceiling, creating space in your hip socket. Your leg should feel free to move within your hip joint and your breathing should be deep and even as you circle each leg.

▲how's it going?

Now pump your arms up and down as before. Aim to build up to 100 pumps. Lowering the legs to a 45-degree angle further increases the challenge to the abdominals.

To finish, bend your knees back toward your body, lower your head to the floor, and then place your feet, one at a time, back onto the floor.

To move into Leg Circles, inhale and extend one leg out until it is flat on the floor. Exhale and repeat with the other leg until both legs are fully extended and you are lying flat.

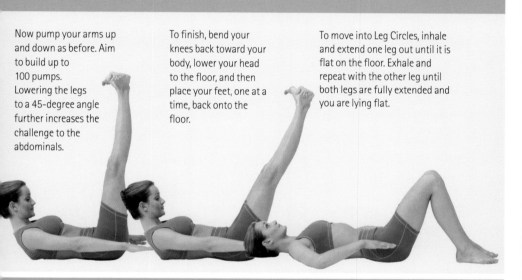

Exhale and repeat the movement, traveling in the same direction. Repeat five times, inhaling for one circle, exhaling for the next. Then circle the same leg five times in the opposite direction, breathing as above.

Keep your pelvis stable, your lower back still, and your neck and shoulders relaxed. Keep your knees extended, feeling your hamstring muscles stretching out. You may also need to keep the back of your knees soft, rather than locked.

To move into the Side Lift, roll over onto your side, placing one arm underneath your head and the other on the floor in front of your ribs. Stretch your legs out, slightly ahead of your body.

▶▶

2

side lift & bicycle on side

The Side Lift strengthens the stabilizer muscles along one side of the spine. The Bicycle provides unilateral support, and also stretches the psoas—the deep postural muscle that connects the lumbar spine to the legs.

SIDE LIFT—BEGINNER LEVEL

15

Start in the position described at the end of Leg Circles. Inhale and lengthen out of your waist, feeling how the inhalation automatically elongates the spine and gently lifts your hips off the floor.

Exhale. Lift both legs off the floor while maintaining length through the entire spine. Keep the right shoulder directly above the left one, and the right hip directly above the left one.

Hold the lift for a count of five before you inhale and lower your legs back down. At all times, maintain the length through the back, waist, neck, and legs.

BICYCLE ON SIDE—INTERMEDIATE LEVEL

16

Rest on your left side, with your left knee bent at a 90-degree angle in front of you, and your left elbow, lower arm, and left hip supporting your weight.

Keep your left shoulder held steady by spreading your weight down and across your back, opening up your ribs on the left side.

Stretch your right leg out in line with your hip, flex your foot and reach through the heel. Move the crown of your head away in the opposite direction.

how's it going?

Most of us tend to use one side of the body more than the other and are therefore stronger and more stable on that side. The Side Lift is a great way to find out which side is the more stable, while strengthening any weakness at the same time. When practicing the Bicycle on Side, you should feel lengthened throughout the entire side of the body you are working on.

⬆how's it going?

Once you touch the floor, start the next Side Lift on the exhale. Repeat this exercise six to eight times. After the last repetition, keep your legs raised, ready for the second part of the exercise.

Lower your bottom leg to just above the floor. Exhale, and squeeze the legs back together. Repeat this action six to eight times. To finish, inhale, and lower both legs back down. Exhale, roll onto your right side. and repeat the entire sequence.

To move into Bicycle on Side, roll back onto your left side. Bend your left knee in at a 90-degree angle underneath you and bring yourself up onto your left elbow, carrying the weight on your lower arm.

On an inhalation, bend your knee slightly, and slightly flex your lower back. On an exhalation, extend your heel away, and move it in a large circle behind you, fully extending your hip. Keep the crown of your head pointed in the opposite direction.

Without losing any hip extension, or arching your lower back further, bend your knee further and continue the circle further behind you with your foot. Inhale and bring your knee forward while curving your back. Circle your leg in front of you.

Repeat three to five times on each side. Move into Double Leg Stretches by lowering yourself back down onto the floor, rolling onto your back, and bending your knees into your chest, placing your hands onto your knees.

▶▶

2

double & single leg stretches 1

Both the Leg Stretches are classic Pilates exercises designed to strengthen the anterior abdominal wall using deep breathing and the weight of your legs as levers to increase the abdominal work.

DOUBLE LEG STRETCHES—ALL LEVELS

17

Inhale and bend one knee into your body so that your shin is parallel to the floor with your foot softly pointed. Exhale and bend the other knee in the same way until both knees are in line with your hips. Place one hand on each knee, with your elbows bent out to the side.

Inhale, and curl your shoulders down toward your hips, rolling your head forward until your chin is just above your breastbone and your eyes are focused into your navel.

Drawing your abdominal muscles into your spine, exhale, and extend both arms and legs simultaneously at a 45-degree angle to the floor.

SINGLE LEG STRETCHES 1—ALL LEVELS

18

Starting from the position in which you completed the previous exercise, inhale and bend one knee into your body until your knee is above your hip and your shin is parallel to the floor.

Exhale and repeat with your other leg until both knees are in line with your hips, feet softly pointed.

Inhale and roll your head forward until your chin is above your breastbone and your neck is long. Keep your shoulder blades anchored and drawn down under the armpits.

how's it going?

Double Leg Stretches involves a good degree of coordination as well as muscular strength. Remember to draw your abdominals in as you perform the exercise. When performing Single Leg Stretches, try to coordinate your movements so that as one leg is bending the other leg is already preparing to extend. Your breathing should be a short inhalation followed by a longer exhalation as the leg extends. Think of sniffing the short breath in through your nose and blowing the longer breath out through your mouth.

⬆how's it going?

WARNING: DO NOT PERFORM THIS EXERCISE IF YOU HAVE A NECK DISORDER.

Reach your arms past your knees, as if reaching toward the opposite wall, drawing your shoulders down. Straighten your knees and softly point your toes. Inhale and pause for one second.

Exhale as you reach your arms behind you, level with your ears, and circle your arms around until they reach past your knees again. Inhale as you hold the position. Exhale as you roll your head back

down and bend your knees in, placing your hands back on your knees with your elbows out to the side and shoulders down. Relax. Repeat the entire movement six to 10 times, then lower one foot at a time back to the floor.

Exhale, and extend your left leg from the knee, placing both hands on your right knee, which is still bent. Keep your elbows out to the side and your shoulders drawn down.

Soften your ribs into the floor and feel your back open. Your extended leg should be above the level of the hip so that there is no strain or arching in the lower back.

If your back wants to arch, lift your leg higher until the strain is removed.

▶▶

2

single leg stretches 2 & criss cross

Single Leg Stretches 2 continues the work from the previous page. Criss Cross is an original Pilates exercise that strengthens the oblique abdominals and stabilizes the lower trunk. It also trains upper and lower body coordination.

SINGLE LEG STRETCHES 2—ALL LEVELS

19

Inhale as you bend your left knee in toward your body.

Exhale as you extend your right leg, this time placing your hands on your left knee and pressing your abdominals into your spine.

Keep your neck lengthened and your eyes looking straight ahead between your knees.

CRISS CROSS—INTERMEDIATE LEVEL

20

Inhale, drawing your abdominals in, and dropping your shoulders down. Exhale as you extend your right leg. As you do so, twist your upper body so that the elbow of your right arm crosses over, toward your bent left knee.

Keep your abdominals drawn into your spine and your shoulders open across your back. Make sure that the twist occurs below the shoulder blade, rather than just from the shoulders themselves, and keep your neck muscles relaxed.

Inhale as you come back to center, passing through your original starting position—both knees bent with your head pointing forward toward your knees.

how's it going?

If, at the end of the Leg Stretches, your neck feels tense, ignore the transition straight into Criss Cross and use this as a point to take a rest. When performing Criss Cross, take care not to pull on your neck with your hands, as this can be dangerous. Your head should feel as if it is resting comfortably in your hands. Keep your middle, lower back, and pelvis stable throughout the movement, only twisting through your upper body. Don't overarch your lower back. Beginners should start by keeping their feet on the floor and twisting their upper body only.

⌃how's it going?

Repeat 10 to 20 times, depending on your level of fitness, then repeat on the other leg.

To move into Criss Cross, finish the exercise with both knees bent toward you, your shins parallel to the floor and your upper body and head up.

With your fingers clasped together, place your hands behind your head. You are now ready for the Criss Cross.

WARNING: AVOID THIS EXERCISE IF YOU SUFFER FROM A DISORDER OF THE NECK OR LOWER BACK.

Exhale as you extend your left leg, this time twisting your upper body so that your left elbow moves toward your right knee.

Alternate five times on each side as if pedaling a bicycle. Exhale on each extension of each leg, and inhale as you pass through center.

To move into Roll Over, inhale and roll back down. Extend your arms out along your body. Exhale and put your feet down. Inhale and extend both legs out. Exhale, and press your hands gently into the floor.

▶▶

3

roll over & spine stretch

Roll Over mobilizes the entire spine and stretches the back muscles. The most valuable aspect of the Spine Stretch is that it addresses posture. You really have to make an effort to sit upright and balance the spine in a vertical position.

ROLL OVER—ALL LEVELS

21

Lie on your back with knees bent, your feet on the floor, and your arms alongside your body. Inhale, and bend your right knee and then your left toward your body, until your shins are parallel to the floor, and your knees are above your hips.

Exhale and draw your abdominals in as you extend your legs up toward the ceiling, straightening them only as far as is comfortable. Keep your pelvis neutral and don't arch your lower back.

Pause and inhale to prepare to roll over. Exhaling slowly, let your legs travel toward your face until you have rolled onto your shoulders (not your neck).

SPINE STRETCH (WITH EXTENSION)—INTERMEDIATE LEVEL

22

Sit up as tall as you can, with your legs in front of you and feet shoulder-width apart. Point your toes at the ceiling. Lengthen your arms out in front of you, making sure that your shoulders are relaxed.

Inhale, internally lengthening through your spine. As you exhale, start curving the crown of your head toward the floor.

Continue moving your spine into a curve, making sure that your pelvis is vertical. On an inhalation, gradually straighten your spine into a diagonal line, starting from the tailbone and finishing with the crown of the head.

how's it going?

Roll Over is not a beginner's exercise so when you attempt it for the first time, keep your knees bent and roll over only as far as is comfortable. If you are new to the movement, keep your knees bent. As you get stronger, you should aim to have your legs completely straight throughout the exercise. The most important aspect of the Spine Stretch is the length through the spine. If your hamstrings are short, your lower back tight, and you find yourself unable to sit upright, try sitting on a telephone book, or similar, to avoid the pelvis tilting back and the spine shortening.

▲how's it going?

WARNING: DO NOT ATTEMPT THIS EXERCISE IF YOU SUFFER FROM A NECK OR SPINAL DISK INJURY.

Keep your arms stretched down by your sides and your abdominals pulled in toward your spine to support it.

Inhale then exhale as you roll back until your feet are pointing to the ceiling. Repeat six times, then bend your knees back in and

place your feet back onto the floor. To move into Spine Stretch, roll your head forward and sit up so your back is straight, then extend your legs out in front of you.

On the next exhale, gently lower your head, allowing your spine to curve, and bring your pelvis back to vertical.

Imagine the next inhalation traveling from the base of your spine up to the crown of your head and stack your spine, vertebra by vertebra, up to vertical.

Repeat four to six times. If making a diagonal line with your back feels awkward, leave that part out and just stay with a simple curve that then straightens back up.

▶▶

3

saw & spine twist

The Saw improves posture and stabilizes the shoulder girdle. The Spine Twist stabilizes the pelvis while rotating and lengthening the spine. As with all Pilates exercises, it increases the support from the core abdominal muscles.

SAW—INTERMEDIATE LEVEL

23

Sit up with your legs extended out in front of you, feet slightly wider than your hips. Flex your feet and press your heels into the floor. Extend your arms out and sit up as tall as you can.

Inhale and twist to your left. Reach both arms away from your body, keeping your pelvis stable.

Exhale and lean forward, reaching your right hand past your left foot so that it "saws" past the little toe of that foot. Turn to look up toward the left.

SPINE TWIST—BEGINNER TO INTERMEDIATE LEVEL

24

Sit up straight but draw your legs together so that your inner thighs are pressed together. Keep your feet flexed and your heels pressed into the floor.

Lengthen your legs and make sure that you are sitting so that the weight of your body falls directly over your sitting bones.

Extend your arms out to the side with one palm facing back. Inhale, then as you exhale, twist to the right, pulsing twice.

how's it going?

When performing the Saw, if you have tight hamstrings or a weak lower back and find it difficult to sit upright without gripping at the hips or straining your lower back, sit on a large book so that you are raised off the floor. The aim is to keep your legs straight and your back upright without tension. With the Spine Twist, if your shoulders are too tight to keep them relaxed while your arms are fully extended, try doing the exercise with your hands clasped behind your head.

⏶how's it going?

Inhale and sit back up, still on a diagonal, drawing your abdominals in to help lift you up out of your hips. One hand should reach as far away as it can from the other.

Exhale and return to center, your arms out to your sides, your ribs relaxed, and your back straight. Repeat, twisting and leaning forward to the right side.

Alternate the exercise, five on each side, lengthening your legs and reaching your heels forward. Try not to tense the front of your thighs.

Keep your arms extended and make sure that your left arm does not come forward and that your pelvis remains still with your weight evenly distributed.

Inhale to return to center, your arms outstretched, your legs long and your back upright.

Repeat, twisting to the left, exhaling as you twist and pulse. Reach your fingertips away from each other to feel the stretch in your shoulder blades.

▸▸

3

teaser 2 & preparation for control back

Teaser 2 is one of a series of classical abdominal exercises that strengthen the abdominals and hip flexors, while testing balance. The Control Back exercise strengthens the triceps muscles in the upper arm and the back of the body.

TEASER 2—INTERMEDIATE TO ADVANCED

25

On an exhalation, curve your lower spine and bend your knees toward your chest and find your balance with your feet off the floor. On an inhalation, stretch your legs out in front, off the ground, and reach your hands toward your ankles.

From this point, try to keep your balance throughout and be careful not to let your back sag.

You can assist your balance in this position by keeping your shoulders anchored wide and down into the back, balancing the head and neck softly on top, and scooping in your abdominals.

PREPARATION FOR CONTROL BACK—INTERMEDIATE LEVEL

26

Sit up with your knees bent in front of you. Place your hands behind you, with fingers pointing forward.

As you exhale, shift your weight onto your hands and feet, and lift your pelvis until you have created a "table top" shape with your body. Keep your pelvis level and hip sockets open and hold for five breaths before you lower back down.

Support your weight by using the whole length of your arms, not just your shoulders. Bring your pelvis up, inhale, and as you exhale, extend your right leg forward in line with the other knee.

how's it going?

If you cannot keep your balance with Teaser 2, or if the exercise hurts your hip flexors, back, neck, or shoulders, place your elbows behind your pelvis and rest on your forearms. Keep your pelvis curled under and scoop your abdomen deep into your spine. Then perform the same action as below with the legs. Try not to change the position of the pelvis. The Control Back exercise shown here has been adapted from the classical version and is suitable for any level.

⬆how's it going?

On the next exhalation, lower your legs a few inches. Inhale and lift your legs back up using your abdominals. It is extremely important to use your abdominals here and not your hip flexors, which can easily be damaged.

Also ensure that your lower back does not change position during this movement.

Repeat the lower and lift five to 10 times. After the last leg lift, bend your knees and exhale to place your feet back down on the floor. Relax your muscles.

Inhale, bend your left knee and place your foot back on the ground. Exhale and extend your right leg in line with your left knee.

Repeat the sequence four to eight times on each leg then lower your pelvis back down.

To move into Mermaid, allow your knees to fall to the left and transfer your weight over to your left hand and left foot.
This makes a quarter turn toward the left.

▶▶

3

mermaid & prone hamstring curls

The Mermaid shown here strengthens and lengthens the side of the body. Hamstring Curls isolates the buttock (gluteus) muscles and the hamstrings to stretch the hip muscles.

MERMAID—INTERMEDIATE LEVEL

27

With your right arm on your shin and your left arm stretched out to the side with your fingertips reaching down to the floor, start a long inhalation through your nose, and, focusing on your right fingertips, reach out and toward the right.

Continue to inhale and reach your right hand up over your head. At the end of the inhalation, shift your weight onto your left hand and your feet, lifting the weight off your hips, and come up into a long sideways arc.

Support your weight by using the whole length of your arm, not just your shoulder. Exhale as you gradually lower your hips back down to the floor, softening the knees and taking the weight off your hands and feet.

PRONE HAMSTRING CURLS—BEGINNER LEVEL

28

Lie face down with your forehead resting on your hands, your neck long, and your legs lengthened. On an inhalation, bend your right knee until your foot points up to the ceiling. Try to engage only your hamstring. Keep your hip socket and lower back long and your pelvis still.

As you exhale, increase the hip stretch by just lifting your right knee off the ground slightly. Watch that the left side of your pelvis remains still on the floor.

On an inhalation, straighten the right knee while keeping the hip stretched.

how's it going?

When performing the Mermaid, ensure that your body remains sideways and avoid rotation. If the exercise hurts your wrist or shoulder, make sure that your shoulder blade reaches down and away from your spine. If the exercise is still too hard on your wrist, support yourself on your entire lower arm and elbow once you lift your hips off the floor. When starting Prone Hamstring Curls, imagine that your buttock muscles gently engage, the muscles of your lower back and abdominals lengthen, and that your spine is subsequently lengthened.

⬆how's it going?

On the next inhalation, stretch your left arm out to the side and reach all the way over to the right, stretching the left side of your body.

Exhale as you bring your arms back over your head, your torso to vertical, and return to your starting position. Repeat the exercise three or four times on each side.

To move into Prone Hamstring Curls, let yourself slide down onto your side and roll onto the front of your body, placing your hands on top of each other, underneath your forehead. Bend your elbows out to the side.

As you exhale, keep reaching out through the top of the foot and lower the leg back down to the floor.

Repeat the same action on the other leg. Do five to seven repetitions on each leg.

Remain in this position to move into Diamond Press.

▶▶

diamond press & cat stretch

The Diamond Press strengthens the back extensors and hamstrings, and lengthens the abdominals and hip flexors. The Cat Stretch eases the spine and acts as a balance for the Prone Hamstring Curls and the Diamond Press.

DIAMOND PRESS—INTERMEDIATE TO ADVANCED

29

Start by lying face down with your forehead resting on your hands.

Elongate your spine and lengthen your legs and toes away from you. While breathing in, press your hands into the floor, lengthening your spine to its

fullest extent.
While breathing out, bring your right foot, which is controlled from the back of your leg, up to the ceiling.

CAT STRETCH—ALL LEVELS

30

Inhale into your back, lengthening your belly along the front of your body, elongating through your head and neck. On an exhalation, start reaching your arms forward, directing your focus out and along the floor and allow your pelvis to come off your heels.

Still exhaling, travel further forward, reaching up and back with the sitting bones in your buttocks and reaching forward and out with your chest. Keep your focus moving out as well.

Make sure your shoulder blades spread wide across your back by keeping your hands shoulder-width apart and rolling your biceps up to the ceiling.

how's it going?

When performing the Diamond Press, try to ensure that you keep lengthening your hip sockets while pushing your breastbone forward and upward to reduce strain on your lower back—the key to back extension is to project through your breastbone. The Cat Stretch is derived from yoga, where it is known as the Cat Cow. In the Cat Stretch, you will move fluently from flexing muscle to extending muscle, with the emphasis on opening your upper spine and chest. This exercise also opens up your shoulders.

⬆how's it going?

Breathe in, elongating your hip socket control to lower your foot back down to the ground.

Repeat the same sequence with your left leg and make sure that there is no shift in your pelvis. Repeat each leg exercise three to five times, alternating left and right legs as you do so.

While breathing in, bring both heels up to the ceiling and, when breathing out, press yourself higher on your hands while trying to lift your knees off the floor.

When you have reached your full extension, inhale deeply and elongate the arch of your spine even further. Keep your focus going forward and out with your chest, while keeping your pelvis reaching back.

On an exhalation, start curling your tailbone under and bring your pelvis back onto your heels. As you inhale, roll your spine back up to vertical, vertebra by vertebra, until you are sitting tall with your hands on your thighs. Repeat as necessary.

To move into Preparation for Control Front, come up onto all fours. Make sure your hands are directly underneath your shoulders and that your knees are underneath your hips.

▶▶

3

preparation for, & control front

Preparation for Control Front not only helps to prepare for Control Front, but also addresses some aspects of its own. The exercise strengthens the shoulder girdle and is a demanding exercise to perform.

PREPARATION FOR CONTROL FRONT—BEGINNER TO INTERMEDIATE LEVEL

31

Start on all fours with your knees and ankles together. Check that your shoulders are stable and open across your back, and that your hands are directly underneath your shoulders and your knees are directly underneath your hips.

As you exhale, curl your tailbone under, rounding your back up to the ceiling. Keep your head and neck relaxed and in line with the curve of your spine.

As you inhale, tuck your toes under, spread your shoulder blades further across your back, and lift your knees 1 in. (2.5 cm) off the floor.

CONTROL FRONT—ADVANCED LEVEL

32

From the push-up position, inhale to prepare, then exhale as you kick your left leg up behind you to the ceiling. Support your weight by using the whole length of your arms, not just your shoulders.

Keep your toes pointing away from you and your pelvis stable so that you do not drop your left hip. Pulse once and flex your foot, reaching your heel further up to the ceiling.

Inhale as you lower your left leg to the floor, and then exhale as you repeat the kicking movement with your right leg.

how's it going?

Preparation for Control Front makes deep use of the abdominals, the buttock muscles (*gluteus medius* in particular), and the muscles in the front of the thigh (the *quadriceps*). It does require quite a lot of strength to perform, but it also builds strength, so try to work to your full capacity. Try not to allow your pelvis to move as you raise your feet. Keep your pelvis stable so that you don't drop either hip as you perform Control Front.

☝how's it going?

Inhale, then as you exhale, lift your right foot off the floor and hold for five counts. As you exhale, place your right foot back down. Repeat the same action with the left foot. Do three to five repetitions on each side.

To finish, inhale and lower your knees back down to the floor. As you exhale move your toes along the floor and your spine back into the table-top position.

To move into Control Front, step your legs back, one by one, out to the back, keeping your toes curled under, until you are in a push-up position. Holding this position is an exercise in its own right.

Keep your neck long, in line with your shoulders, and draw your shoulder blades down to keep them free of tension.

Do this five times on each side, alternating each time.

Alternating each side challenges your stability and prevents you from leaning all your weight on the supporting side.

▶▶

elephant stretch & push up

The Elephant Stretch lengthens the spine, opens the shoulders, and stretches the hamstrings and calf muscles. The Push Up stabilizes and strengthens the shoulders and works down to the hamstrings. It also strengthens the triceps in the arms.

ELEPHANT STRETCH—ALL LEVELS

33

From the last position of the previous exercise, reach your sitting bones diagonally behind you, pushing yourself up onto your hands and knees.

Ensure that you carry equal weight through your wrists and palms, and think of rolling your biceps gently forward.

Your shoulder blades should spread out wide across your back, without thrusting your ribs or straining your neck.

PUSH UP—ADVANCED LEVEL

34

From the plank-like position described above, hold your body steady, inhale, and bend your arms so that your body is lowered toward the floor.

Only lower yourself as far as you can support yourself. The bending of your arms will probably be small to begin with. Exhale as you straighten your arms, pushing back up to the starting position.

Keep your gluteals and hamstrings working to help stabilize your pelvis and lower spine.

how's it going?

The Elephant Stretch is derived from the Down Dog posture in yoga. Joseph Pilates translated the Down Dog into an exercise that could be performed with his best-known piece of equipment, the "Reformer." When performed on the floor, as shown here, without equipment, the Elephant is much like the original Down Dog. When doing the Push Up, don't put too much weight through your wrists, but think of your body weight being held centrally.

⏶how's it going?

Try to lengthen your spine back along a straight diagonal, and if your heels are off the floor, walk your feet in a little.

Create as much length as possible through your spine and the backs of your legs by actively working the position for five breaths. If it is too hard on the wrists, come out of the position each time and start again.

To move into the next position, walk your hands forward into an upper Push Up (also referred to as the "plank" position).

After three to eight repetitions, walk your hands back toward your feet and unroll the spine to standing on the exhale.

Repeat this exercise two or three times by rolling back down from standing and walking your hands back out until you are in the "plank" position again.

▶▶

4

standing roll down & shoulder curl

Standing Roll Down is a gentle spinal rotation, opening the chest and shoulders, and stretching the backs of the legs. Shoulder Curl provides a release through the shoulders, taking the shoulder joint through a range of extension and rotation.

STANDING ROLL DOWN (WITH SPINAL ROTATION)—ALL LEVELS

35

Inhale and stand up tall, making sure that your feet are wide and your shoulders and neck are relaxed.

Exhale and start rolling the crown of your head toward the floor, into a full forward bend.

Remain in the forward bend and, on an inhalation, bend your right knee while opening your left arm to the ceiling. Feel the stretch in the back of your left leg.

SHOULDER CURL (INTO STANDING)—ALL LEVELS

36

Inhale, and reach your fingertips behind you and continue circling them up to the ceiling. Your palms should now face toward the front.

On the next exhalation, keep reaching your fingertips up to the ceiling, while slowly unrolling your spine, vertebra by vertebra, back up to vertical.

Make sure you start the "unrolling" from the base of the spine, not leaving out any part of your back.

how's it going?

The Standing Roll Down exercise shown here is a variation on the basic technique demonstrated at the start of the program (see pp. 54–55). It is suitable for both the warming-up and the unwinding sections of your Pilates practice. The Shoulder Curl will also provide a final release through the spine.

⌃how's it going?

On the next exhalation, gently straighten both legs and return your left hand back down to the floor. Repeat the same action, rotating toward the left.

Repeat the sequence once more on each side. Then either inhale, return to standing, and repeat the sequence again, or proceed straight to the next exercise.

Once you have arrived back at a standing position, with your arms above your head, inhale, and lower your arms in front of you until they are by your side.

You can repeat this exercise once more, if you feel you need to, or finish the sequence here.

▶▶

continuing your practice

Now that you've been introduced to this program for beginners, you might wonder where to go next. Any exercise program needs adjusting and changing at some point. If you feel you're getting bored then that is a good time to visit a Pilates studio and try out some equipment, or to check out an advanced matwork class or book.

Where possible, it is preferable to begin Pilates practice under the guidance of a qualified teacher before starting to work by yourself. The program in this book is designed to work different areas of the body. We're all different, so these exercises will provide different challenges for each individual. You may find there are a few exercises you don't understand, or that

don't feel right for you. You might even think that some are too easy, and that others are too difficult. To answer any questions you might have, and to enrich your technique, you could consider asking for instruction from a certified Pilates teacher.

A teacher is able to explain the Pilates technique in much greater depth. He or she can spot your individual strengths and weaknesses, and can guide you in using your body most efficiently. There are many different organizations that certify Pilates teachers. You can contact one of them to find a teacher in your area. For starters, you can log on to www.pilatesmethodalliance.org.

glossary

abdominals General term used for the four groups of muscles found in and around the abdomen.

Alexander Technique Movement technique devised by F. Matthias Alexander. The key principle of Alexander is to release tension at the point where the base of the skull articulates with, and balances on, the spine (the atlas and axis joint).

biomechanics Relating to the movement mechanics of the anatomical body.

cartilage Shiny, whitish connective tissue, mostly found at articulating surfaces of bones.

center (physical center) Also called the "inner unit" or "power house," the physical center can be created by contracting the abdominals, pelvic floor, and back muscles to create a steady support in the core of the body's trunk. Developing a strong physical center is one of the key principles of Pilates.

cervical Relates to the seven cervical (neck) vertebrae.

core and core stability Underneath all visible movements lie deeper, smaller movements. These smaller movements are performed by deeper muscles, which are referred to as intrinsic muscles. These intrinsic muscles function to stabilize joints, give anchor for mobility, and give favorable posture for optimal movement.

feldenkrais technique Movement technique devised by Moshe Feldenkrais.

gyrokinesis Gyrokinesis relates to all the exercises Juliu Horvath created and brought into sequence that do not involve specialized equipment. Gyrokinesis can be taught in conjunction with, or separate from, Gyrotonic.

gyrotonic Exercise technique devised by Juliu Horvath using specialized equipment. Like Pilates, the technique promotes structural fitness, but its emphasis is on flowing three-dimensional movement and spirals.

intervertebral disk A disk of cartilage located between each vertebrae, which acts as a shock absorber for the spine.

ligaments Dense bundles of parallel collagenous fibers that connect bone to bone and therefore are major stabilizers of joints.

lumbar Relates to the five lumbar (lower back) vertebrae of the spinal column.

multifidus Deep back muscles.

muscles Tissues capable of contraction and relaxation that generate movement in a skeleton or organ.

musculoskeletal Pertaining to, or affecting, both muscles and skeleton.

neuromuscular Pertaining to, or affecting, both muscles and nerves.

neutral spine The maintenance of the three natural curves of the spine in their correct positions. Related to the alignment of the shoulders and pelvis.

occipital Relates to occiput, the cranial bone at the back of the base of the skull.

prone Back of the body facing up.

sacral Relating to the sacrum, the five fused and modified vertebrae that articulate with the pelvic bones, the ilium.

supine Front of the body facing up.

tendons Bands of inelastic fibrous tissues that connect muscle to bone.

thoracic Relates to the 12 thoracic (upper back) vertebrae.

for more information

IDEA Health & Fitness Association
10455 Pacific Center Court
San Diego, CA 92121
(800) 999-4332, ext. 7
Web site: http://www.ideafit.com
This organization provides information about
fitness and wellness professionals and
resources relating to Pilates.

Medical Fitness Association
1905 Huguenot Road, Suite 203
Richmond, VA 23235-8026
(804) 897-5701
Web site: http://www.medicalfitness.org
This nonprofit association works to develop
and operate medically integrated fitness
centers. It provides information on fitness
standards and educational programs.

Pilates Method Alliance
P.O. Box 370906
Miami, FL 33137-0906
(866) 573-4945
Web site: http://www.pilatesmethodalliance.org
This is a professional organization and certifying
agency for Pilates teachers. It also
promotes the Pilates method of exercise.

Power Pilates
Web site: http://www.powerpilates.com
An APOGEE Wellness company, Power
Pilates offers education and training

programs in classical Pilates around
the world.

President's Council on Physical Fitness and Sports
1101 Wootton Parkway, Suite 560
Rockville, MD 20852
(240) 276-9567
Web site: http://www.finess.gov
An advisory committee made up of twenty-five
people appointed by the U.S. president,
the council members promote healthy
lifestyles through programs focused on
fitness, sports, and nutrition.

U.S. Department of Health and Human Services
200 Independence Avenue SW
Washington, DC 20201
(877) 696-6775
Web site: http://www.hhs.gov
This agency of the federal government protects
the health and wellness of all Americans
and provides essential services and
information on fitness and well-being.

WEB SITES
Due to the changing nature of Internet links,
Rosen Publishing has developed an online list
of Web sites related to the subject of this book.
This site is updated regularly. Please use this
link to access the list:

http://www.rosenlinks.com/fctc/pil

for further reading

Aikman, Louise, and Matthew Harvey. *Pilates Step-by-Step* (Skills in Motion). New York, NY: Rosen Publishing, 2011.

Brignell, Roger. *The Pilates Handbook* (A Young Woman's Guide to Health and Well-Being). New York, NY: Rosen Publishing, 2010.

Daniels, Diane. *Pilates Perfect: The Complete Guide to Pilates Exercise at Home*. New York, NY: Random House, 2004.

Ellsworth, Abby. *Pilates Anatomy*. Charlotte, NC: Thunder Bay, 2009.

Herdman, Alan. *The Pilates Directory*. New York, NY: Metro Books, 2009.

Isacowitz, Rael, and Karen Clippinger. *Pilates Anatomy*. Champaign, IL: Human Kinetics, 2011.

Lyon, Daniel. *Complete Book of Pilates for Men: The Lifetime Plan for Strength, Power and Peak Performance*. New York, NY: HarperCollins, 2005.

Massey, Paul. *Anatomy of Pilates*. Berkeley, CA: North Atlantic Books, 2009.

Nathan, Amy. *Meet the Dancers: From Ballet, Broadway, and Beyond*. New York, NY: Henry Holt, 2008.

Page, Portia. *Pilates Illustrated*. Champaign, IL: Human Kinetics, 2011.

Robinson, Lynne, Lisa Bradshaw, and Nathan Gardner. *The Pilates Bible*. Richmond Hill, ON, Canada: Firefly Books, 2010.

Smith, Judy, Emily Kelly, and Jonathan Monks. *Pilates and Yoga*. New York, NY: Metro Books, 2006.

Ungaro, Alycea. *15 Minute Everyday Pilates*. New York, NY: DK, 2007.

index

ABOUT THE AUTHORS

Sian Williams started teaching Pilates in 1987 and has owned and managed the Pilates Off The Square studio in London, England, with coauthor Dominique Jansen since 1997. She is also a member of the Pilates Foundation UK, the United Kingdom's governing body for the profession.

Dominique Jansen studied dance before starting to teach Pilates in 1989. She is the co-owner and comanager of Pilates Off The Square, in London, where she runs the studio's Pilates teacher training course. She is a board member of the Pilates Foundation UK and a member of the Pilates Foundation UK teacher training committee.